Better Homes and Gardens®

20 MINUTES TO DINNER

Our seal assures you that every recipe in *20 Minutes to Dinner*
has been tested in the Better Homes and Gardens® Test Kitchen.
This means that each recipe is practical and reliable, and
meets our high standards of taste appeal.

BETTER HOMES AND GARDENS® BOOKS
Editor: Gerald M. Knox
Art Director: Ernest Shelton
Managing Editor: David A. Kirchner
Editorial Project Managers: James D. Blume, Marsha Jahns,
    Rosanne Weber Mattson, Mary Helen Schiltz

Department Head, Cook Books: Sharyl Heiken
Associate Department Heads: Sandra Granseth,
    Rosemary C. Hutchinson, Elizabeth Woolever
Senior Food Editors: Julia Malloy, Marcia Stanley, Joyce Trollope
Associate Food Editors: Linda Henry, Mary Major, Diana McMillen,
    Mary Jo Plutt, Maureen Powers, Martha Schiel,
    Linda Foley Woodrum
Test Kitchen: Director, Sharon Stilwell; Photo Studio Director:
    Janet Pittman; Home Economists: Lynn Blanchard, Jean Brekke,
    Kay Cargill, Marilyn Cornelius, Jennifer Darling,
    Maryellyn Krantz, Lynelle Munn, Dianna Nolin, Marge Steenson

Associate Art Directors: Linda Ford Vermie, Neoma Alt West,
    Randall Yontz
Assistant Art Directors: Lynda Haupert, Harijs Priekulis,
    Tom Wegner
Senior Graphic Designers: Jack Murphy, Stan Sams,
    Darla Whipple-Frain
Graphic Designers: Mike Burns, W. Blake Welch, Brian Wignall,
    Kimberly Zarley
Art Production: Director, John Berg;
    Associate, Joe Heuer; Office Manager, Emma Rediger

President, Book Group: Fred Stines
Vice President, Retail Marketing: Jamie Martin
Vice President, Direct Marketing: Arthur Heydendael

BETTER HOMES AND GARDENS® MAGAZINE
Vice President, Editorial Director: Doris Eby
Executive Director, Editorial Services: Duane L. Gregg
Food and Nutrition Editor: Nancy Byal

20 MINUTES TO DINNER
Editor: Mary Jo Plutt
Editorial Project Manager: Mary Helen Schiltz
Graphic Designers: Harijs Priekulis, Kimberly Zarley
Electronic Text Processor: Paula Forest
Food Stylist: Janet Pittman
Contributing Food Stylist: Pat Godsted
Contributing Photographers: Wm. Hopkins, Scott Little,
    Kathy Sanders
Contributing Illustrator: Thomas Rosborough

On the front cover: Broiled Chicken Cordon Bleu
(see recipe, page 22)

Good cooking has to take time—or so I thought before I started writing *20 Minutes to Dinner*. Then, if I needed a quick meal, I'd pick up burgers or a pizza on the way home from work.

Now, I'm happy to say, I've become a 20-minute cook. And rather than buying takeout, I enjoy Broiled Chicken Cordon Bleu, Shrimp Étouffée, or Skillet Fajitas.

What changed my mind? It was the many cooking, shopping, and menu-planning shortcuts I discovered while developing recipes for *20 Minutes to Dinner*. In each recipe, I've built in a lot of these work- and timesaving ideas. Plus, I've included three menus that'll help you solve those last-minute, what's-for-dinner problems.

So the next time you need dinner in a hurry, try a quick-to-fix recipe from this book. You'll soon discover, as I did, that good cooking doesn't have to take time. Just set your timer for 20 minutes and see!

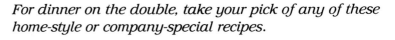
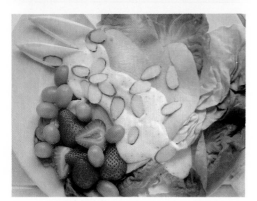
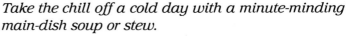

Hearty Sandwiches 55

Satisfy hungry appetites with one of our many hot or cold sandwiches.

Make-Ahead Freezer Mix 63

Base a jiffy dinner on this handy mix.

Mealtime Extras 69

Round out your meals with one of our speedy side dishes, breads, and desserts.

Index 79

Invest in Convenience

These work-saving ingredients may cost a little more, but they're a profitable investment for last-minute meals.

- Deli-cooked beef, turkey breast, *and* ham
- Cooked bacon pieces
- Frozen diced cooked chicken
- Boned, skinless, fresh chicken breast halves
- Fresh turkey breast tenderloins
- Canned, boneless, skinless pink salmon
- Deli crab-flavored fish sticks
- Deli-made salads (see tip, page 51)
- In-supermarket salad bar lettuce mixtures (see tip, page 48) *and* precut fresh vegetables
- Preshredded fresh cabbage
- Frozen chopped onion *and* green pepper (see tip, page 12)
- Frozen snipped chives
- Bottled minced garlic
- Bottled lemon juice
- Quick-cooking rice *and* couscous
- Baking powder biscuits *and* corn bread from the bakery
- Broken nuts
- Presliced *and* preshredded cheese
- Deli hard-cooked eggs (see tip, page 56)

It's 5:30, you've just arrived home, and you need to leave again by 6:30. That gives you 1 hour to cook dinner for your family, eat, and cleanup.

Sound familiar? In the next two pages we'll show you how to win this great dinner race without wearing yourself to a frazzle. Just read through these pointers before you head for the kitchen.

Menu Planning

The key to preparing meals in a hurry is organization.
- Plan several days of menus at once, using leftovers from one meal in the next. For example, use leftover cooked meats and poultry in soups, stews, salads, or sandwiches. Or, use up small amounts of uncooked meats and vegetables in stir-fries.
- Serve only two- or three-course meals. Team a meat-and-vegetable main dish with a salad, or skip the salad and opt for a dessert.
- Use a purchased item for one of the courses. Keep frozen yogurt or ice cream, or canned pudding on hand for dessert. And for easy last-minute salads, serve a wedge of iceberg lettuce with bottled dressing. Or, stop at the deli and select whatever you need to round out a meal.

Shopping Tips

Shopping efficiently is another way to save time.
- As you're planning menus, check your kitchen shelves, refrigerator, and freezer. If you're running low on any staples, replace them *before* you run out.
- Once your meals are planned, make a master grocery list and do all of your shopping at once. This way you can skip the hassle of last-minute shopping trips.
- Shop at markets you're familiar with so you don't waste time looking for items.
- Avoid "rush hour" at the supermarket. Pick a time to shop when the aisles aren't crowded and checkout lines are short.
- Eliminate unnecessary backtracking at the store by grouping the items on your list by categories, such as meats, dairy products, produce, canned goods, cereals, frozen foods, nonfood items, and baked goods.
- Buy ingredients in the form you'll need them for cooking. (See tip at left.)

Storage Strategy

Spend just a few extra minutes putting away groceries, and you'll save lots of time before dinner.
- Stack individual ground meat patties, steaks, or chops between two layers of waxed paper. Then slip them into a moisture- and vaporproof bag. Seal, label, and freeze.

To use, simply remove the number of pieces you need—without prying them apart.
- Slice a loaf of French bread to, *but not through,* the

... Go!!!

bottom crust. Spread the cut edges with softened butter or margarine, or with a spread from page 70. Then wrap the loaf in foil, label, and freeze.

To serve, heat the foil-wrapped loaf in the oven while you're making the main dish.

● Divide rolls, muffins, and breads into meal-size portions before freezing. At mealtime, just thaw out as many as you need.

● Prepare ingredients for several recipes at one time. For example, chop extra vegetables, cook a double batch of pasta and rice, or hard-cook several eggs. (See tips, pages 12 and 56.)

● Chill cans of fruits, vegetables, or meats for salads so they're ready when you need them.

Kitchen Organization

A well-equipped and organized kitchen can also reduce KP duty.

● Arrange your kitchen so you can find things quickly. Keep utensils close to where they're used. For example, store pots and pans near the stove, and keep sharp knives near the the cutting board.

● Always store frequently used items in the same place. This way, you won't have to hunt for them.

● Turn labels on cans or boxes toward the front so you'll be able to read them at a glance.

20 MIN TO DINNER

Dinner, pronto, is as simple as 1, 2, 3, 4—if you follow our four-step strategy.

1 The night before
● Place frozen meat, fish, or seafood in the refrigerator to thaw.
● Read the recipe and check your pantry to make sure you have all of the ingredients you'll need. If you're missing something, check our emergency substitution chart—Making a Quick Switch—on page 38.

2 As you start cooking
● Preheat the broiler or oven, reread the recipe, and gather all of the ingredients and utensils you'll need.

3 During cooking
● If you can, always do two things at once. For example, while water is boiling for the pasta, open cans or chop vegetables.

● Hurry up heating by choosing wide-diameter saucepans.
● To boil water, start with *hot* tap water.
● Use work- and timesaving ingredients and gadgets whenever possible to speed up preparation. (See tips, opposite and on page 48.)
● Cut down on cleanup by reusing measuring cups and spoons. Measure dry ingredients before the wet ones.
● Have the whole family pitch in. Divide the meal into parts and give each member something to prepare. For example, a child can set the table while Mom and Dad prepare a main dish and a salad or dessert.
● Bake or chill the dessert while you're eating. Doing it then will save you another 30 minutes.

4 Sit down, eat, and enjoy!
You've done it. A delicious meal in just 20 minutes.

MENUS

H

Help is on the way! Next time you have unexpected company, family members eating at different times, or a summer day that's too hot for cooking, rely on a menu from the next three pages to get you out of your dinnertime dilemma.

Too Hot To Cook

Italian Tortellini Salad (see recipe, page 53)
Corn muffins *or* **Italian bread with basil-flavored spread** (see tip, page 70)
Ice cream with desired ice-cream topping
Cookies (optional)
Iced tea *or* **lemonade**

● Prepare flavored spread using basil option.
● For Italian Tortellini Salad, thaw vegetables, cut cheese, and drain olives. Then, combine the salad.
● Before serving, scoop ice cream into dessert bowls. Top the ice cream with your favorite topping.

Entertaining On A Moment's Notice

Orange-Hoisin Sauced
  Poultry (see recipe,
  page 24)
Steamed fresh asparagus
  or broccoli spears
Dark rolls with butter
7-Minute Mocha Mousse
  (see recipe, page 78)
Sparkling water with
  lemon *or* white wine

● For 7-Minute Mocha
Mousse, remove topping from
freezer. Combine milk and
coffee crystals.
● For vegetable, clean spears.
Bring 1½ inches of *hot water*
to boiling in a Dutch oven.
Meanwhile, prepare Orange-
Hoisin Sauced Poultry.
● Place vegetable in a
steamer basket and steam for
3 to 5 minutes or till tender.
● Before serving, finish
preparing mousse.

Vegetable and Cashew
   Soup (see recipe, page 46)
Garlic toast (see tip,
   page 70)
Fresh fruit
Milk

● Preheat broiler. Prepare Vegetable and Cashew Soup.
● For garlic toast, prepare flavored spread using garlic option. Spread mixture onto bread slices, then place on the unheated rack of the broiler pan. Broil till light brown.

● *For latecomers:* Reheat soup over medium-high heat for 2 to 3 minutes or till heated through. Meanwhile, spread bread with garlic mixture; broil.

FAST-FIXING MAIN DISHES

20 MIN

Conquer the what's-for-dinner blues by choosing any of our oh-so-speedy main dishes. Whether you put together a fast-cooking entrée or whip up a one-dish meal, your family and guests will be amazed it took you *less than* 20 minutes!

Double-Duty Chopping

Got a spare minute? Use it to chop an extra onion or green pepper by hand or with a food processor.

Then store it by spreading the chopped onion or green pepper in a single layer in a shallow baking pan and freezing. Next, break the frozen vegetables into pieces and put them into freezer bags or containers. Seal, label, and store them in the freezer for up to 1 month.

To use, just add the amount you need to what you're cooking—no need to thaw!

Cooking-Ahead Pasta and Rice

During the dinner rush, save precious minutes by using your freezer and microwave oven as a helping hand for cooking pasta or long grain rice. You can save up to 12 minutes for pasta and 25 minutes for long grain rice.

● First cook the pasta and rice ahead. (Rinse and drain pasta well.)

Then, for single-serving portions, place ½-cup portions of pasta or rice in 6-ounce custard cups. Cover with clear plastic wrap and freeze for several hours. When frozen, remove the portions from the cups and place them into freezer bags or containers. Seal, label, and store them in the freezer for up to 6 months.

Or, for family-size portions, place 2-cup portions of pasta or rice into freezer bags or containers. Then seal, label, and freeze.

● To reheat single-serving portions, place pasta or rice back into the custard cups. Do *not* add water. Cover with waxed paper. Micro-cook on 100% power (high) until heated through (1½ to 2 minutes for 1 custard cup; 2 to 2½ minutes for 2 custard cups; 4 to 4½ minutes for 4 custard cups).

● To reheat family-size portions, transfer one 2-cup portion of frozen pasta or rice to a medium microwave-safe bowl. Add *2 tablespoons* water. Cover loosely with waxed paper. Micro-cook on 100% power (high) about 5 minutes or till heated, stirring once.

Microwave Power

The recipes in this book were tested in countertop microwave ovens that operate on 600 to 700 watts. Cooking times are approximate since microwave ovens vary by manufacturers.

Curly-Noodle Dinner

Kids love the curly noodles in this home-style beef dish.

1 **pound ground beef** *or* **ground raw turkey sausage**
1 **3-ounce package Oriental noodles with beef** *or* **pork flavor**
1 **14½-ounce can stewed tomatoes**
1 **8-ounce can whole kernel corn**

● Break ground meat into large pieces while adding it to a large skillet. Cook meat over high heat till beef is brown or turkey sausage is no longer pink. Drain off fat.

● Stir in the seasoning packet from the Oriental noodles, *undrained* tomatoes, and *undrained* corn. Then slightly break up noodles while adding them to the meat mixture in the skillet. Stir till combined. Bring mixture to boiling, then reduce heat. Cover and simmer about 10 minutes or till noodles are tender and flavors are blended. Makes 4 or 5 servings.

To micro-cook: Place loose ground beef or turkey sausage in a 2-quart microwave-safe casserole, then cover. Micro-cook on 100% power (high) for 4 to 6 minutes or till meat is no longer pink, stirring once. Drain off fat. Then stir in seasoning packet, *undrained* tomatoes, and *undrained* corn. Slightly break up noodles and stir them into meat mixture. Cook, covered, on high for 8 to 9 minutes or till noodles are tender and flavors are blended, stirring twice.

Pepper Steaks

Pep up the flavor of steak by rubbing it with cracked black pepper.

2 **tablespoons butter** *or* **margarine**
  Cracked black pepper
2 **beef tenderloin steaks, cut 1¼ inches thick (about 10 ounces total)**
12 **small fresh mushroom caps**
1 **tablespoon water**
1 **tablespoon lemon juice**
1 **tablespoon Worcestershire sauce**

● In a large heavy skillet melt butter or margarine. Meanwhile, generously sprinkle cracked pepper over both sides of steaks. (Use about 1 teaspoon of pepper for each steak.) With your fingers, press pepper into steaks.

● Add steaks to skillet and cook over medium-high heat for 6 minutes. Turn steaks over, then add mushroom caps to skillet. Continue cooking over medium-high heat to desired doneness. (Allow 6 to 8 minutes more for medium doneness.) Transfer steaks and mushrooms to dinner plates, then set aside. Remove skillet from the heat.

● For sauce, to the same skillet add water, lemon juice, and Worcestershire sauce. Scrape up brown bits and drippings from bottom of skillet.

● To serve, spoon sauce over the steaks and mushrooms. Makes 2 servings.

Pan-Fried Steaks with Wine

Cinnamon and cloves add a hint of spice.

2 tablespoons butter *or* margarine
2 beef top loin steaks, cut 1 inch thick (about 1½ pounds total)
3 medium green onions
  Salt
  Pepper
⅓ cup dry red wine
  Dash ground cinnamon
  Dash ground cloves

● In a large heavy skillet melt butter or margarine. Cut each steak in half. Add the steaks and cook over medium-high heat for 5 minutes. Turn the steaks over, then continue cooking to desired doneness. (Allow 5 to 7 minutes more for medium doneness.) Meanwhile, slice the green onions, then set aside.

● Sprinkle steaks on both sides with salt and pepper. Then transfer steaks to a serving platter. Cover to keep warm.

● For sauce, in the same skillet cook onions in the drippings over medium-high heat till tender but not brown. Remove the skillet from the heat. Then add the wine, cinnamon, and cloves. Return the skillet to the heat and cook till heated through.

● To serve, spoon sauce over steaks. Makes 4 servings.

Beef 'n' Asparagus Stir-Fry

For fast slicing, use a sharp knife and hold it at a 45-degree angle.

1 cup quick-cooking couscous *or* 1½ cups quick-cooking rice
¾ pound beef flank steak
¼ cup water
2 tablespoons soy sauce
2 tablespoons dry sherry
1½ teaspoons cornstarch
1 teaspoon bottled minced garlic *or* ¼ teaspoon garlic powder
½ teaspoon crushed red pepper
1 tablespoon cooking oil
1 10-ounce package frozen cut asparagus

● Cook couscous or rice according to package directions.

● While couscous or rice is cooking, thinly slice steak on the bias into bite-size strips, then set aside. Preheat a wok or large skillet over high heat.

● While wok is heating, for sauce, in a small mixing bowl or custard cup stir together water, soy sauce, dry sherry, cornstarch, garlic, and red pepper. Set the sauce aside.

● Add oil to hot wok or skillet. (If necessary, add more oil during stir-frying.) Add beef to the wok. Stir-fry over high heat for 2 to 3 minutes or till done. Push beef from center. Break up frozen asparagus while it is still in its package, then add it to center of the wok. Stir-fry for 2 minutes. Push asparagus from center.

● Stir sauce, then add it to the center of the wok. Cook and stir till thickened and bubbly. Cook and stir for 1 minute more. Toss sauce lightly with meat and asparagus to coat. Cook and stir for 1 minute more. Serve over hot couscous or rice. Serves 3 or 4.

Beef 'n' Asparagus
Stir-Fry

Lemon-Mustard Lamb Chops

4 lamb leg sirloin chops, cut ¾ inch thick (about 1 pound total)
2 tablespoons mayonnaise *or* salad dressing
1 tablespoon Dijon-style mustard
1 tablespoon lemon juice
¼ teaspoon dried tarragon, crushed

● Preheat broiler. Meanwhile, place chops on the unheated rack of the broiler pan, then set aside. For mustard mixture, in a small mixing bowl or custard cup stir together mayonnaise or salad dressing, mustard, lemon juice, and tarragon.

● Broil chops 3 inches from the heat for 5 minutes. Brush chops with some of the mustard mixture. Turn chops over and broil to desired doneness. (Allow about 5 minutes more for medium doneness.) Brush the lamb chops with more of the mustard mixture again before serving. Makes 2 servings.

Mid-Eastern-Style Lamb and Couscous

Look for couscous (KOO-skoos), known as Moroccan pasta, near the rice at the supermarket.

8 lamb loin chops, cut ¾ inch thick (about 1½ pounds total)
½ cup frozen chopped onion (see tip, page 12)
1 tablespoon butter *or* margarine
1 cup chicken broth
¼ cup raisins
¼ teaspoon ground cinnamon
⅛ teaspoon ground allspice
Dash ground cumin
¾ cup quick-cooking couscous
2 tablespoons frozen snipped chives

● Preheat broiler. Meanwhile, place chops on the unheated rack of the broiler pan, then set aside. For the couscous mixture, in a medium saucepan cook the frozen onion in butter or margarine over medium-high heat till tender but not brown. Add chicken broth, raisins, cinnamon, allspice, and cumin. Bring to boiling, then remove from heat. Stir in couscous. Cover and let stand for 5 to 7 minutes.

● While couscous is cooking and standing, broil chops 3 inches from the heat for 5 minutes. Turn chops over. Broil to desired doneness. (Allow about 5 minutes more for medium doneness.)

● To serve, stir chives into couscous mixture. Then transfer mixture to a serving platter. Arrange chops on top. Serves 4.

Honey-Mustard Sausage Kabobs

5 fully cooked bratwursts *or* smoked Polish sausages
1 16-ounce can whole new potatoes
2 tablespoons Dijon-style mustard
1 tablespoon honey
Cherry tomatoes (optional)

● Preheat the broiler. Meanwhile, for kabobs, cut each of the bratwursts or Polish sausages crosswise into thirds. Drain the potatoes. Using 3 long skewers, alternately thread the meat and potatoes, leaving about a ¼-inch space between the pieces. Place on the unheated rack of the broiler pan. Combine mustard and honey. Brush kabobs with some of the mixture.

● Broil kabobs 4 inches from the heat for 2 minutes. Turn kabobs over and brush with more honey-mustard mixture. Broil for 2 to 3 minutes more or till heated through. If desired, garnish kabobs with cherry tomatoes. Makes 3 servings.

Picadillo on Rice

Pronounced pee-kah-DEE-yoh, this spicy Spanish sauce is full of meat, raisins, and almonds.

¾ cup quick-cooking rice
8 ounces bulk Italian sausage
¼ cup frozen chopped onion
    (see tip, page 12)
¼ cup frozen chopped green
    pepper (see tip, page 12)
1 15-ounce can tomato sauce
¼ cup slivered almonds
¼ cup raisins
⅛ teaspoon ground cloves
    Dash ground cinnamon
¼ cup drained pitted green
    olives

● Cook rice according to package directions.

● While rice is cooking, prepare picadillo. Break sausage into large chunks while adding it to a large skillet. Cook sausage, frozen onion, and green pepper over high heat till sausage is brown and vegetables are tender. Drain off fat. Stir in tomato sauce, almonds, raisins, cloves, and cinnamon. Bring mixture to boiling, then reduce heat. Simmer, uncovered, for 5 minutes. Then stir in olives. Serve picadillo over hot rice. Serves 2.

To micro-cook: Cook rice in the microwave oven according to package directions. For sauce, place loose sausage, onion, and green pepper in a 1-quart microwave-safe casserole, then cover. Micro-cook on 100% power (high) for 3 to 5 minutes or till sausage is done, stirring once. Drain off fat. Stir in remaining sauce ingredients, *except* olives. Cook, uncovered, on high for 3 to 4½ minutes or till bubbly and heated through, stirring once. Then stir in olives. Serve as above.

Fried Rice with Ham

Turn a side dish into a meal by adding meat and seasonings to canned fried rice.

12 ounces fully cooked
    boneless ham *or* cooked
    boneless beef
2 tablespoons pineapple juice
    or orange juice
½ teaspoon ground ginger
½ teaspoon bottled minced
    garlic *or* ⅛ teaspoon garlic
    powder
⅛ teaspoon onion powder
1 tablespoon butter *or*
    margarine
2 eggs
1 11-ounce can fried rice
½ cup frozen chopped green
    pepper (see tip, page 12)

● Cut meat into cubes (you should have about 2 cups). In a custard cup stir together juice, ginger, garlic, and onion powder.

● In a large skillet melt butter or margarine. Meanwhile, use a fork to slightly beat eggs. Pour into skillet. Cook over medium heat, without stirring, till eggs begin to set on bottom and edges. Then using a spatula, lift and fold partially cooked eggs so the uncooked portions flow underneath. Cook about 1 minute or till eggs are cooked throughout but are still glossy and moist.

● Add meat, juice mixture, rice, and frozen green pepper to eggs in skillet, then cover. Cook over medium heat about 4 minutes or till heated through, stirring occasionally. Serves 3 or 4.

To micro-cook: Cut meat and combine juice mixture as above. Omit butter. In a 1½-quart microwave-safe casserole beat eggs till yolks and whites are well mixed. Micro-cook, uncovered, on 100% power (high) for 30 seconds. Push cooked portions to center. Cook, uncovered, about 30 seconds more or till eggs are *almost* set, pushing cooked portions to center every 15 seconds. Stir in meat, juice mixture, rice, and green pepper. Cover. Cook on high for 4 to 5 minutes or till heated through, stirring twice.

Veggie-Topped Pizza

Add a second topping of veggies and cheese for a hearty pizza fix-up.

1 20- to 22-ounce frozen pizza (about 11½ inches in diameter)
1 cup frozen cut broccoli *or* frozen cauliflower
1 cup shredded mozzarella *or* cheddar cheese (4 ounces)
   Crushed red pepper (optional)
   Grated *or* finely shredded Parmesan cheese (optional)

● Preheat oven to temperature as directed on pizza package.

● Bake frozen pizza on a baking sheet according to the package directions till the last 5 minutes of baking.

● While pizza is baking, cook vegetables according to package directions, then drain. Cut up large pieces. Cover to keep warm.

● Five minutes before pizza is done, spoon hot vegetables on top of pizza, then sprinkle with the mozzarella or cheddar cheese. Return to oven and bake about 5 minutes more or till pizza is done and cheese is melted. If desired, sprinkle with red pepper and Parmesan cheese. Makes 4 servings.

Spinach-Topped Pizza: Prepare the Veggie-Topped Pizza as directed above, *except* substitute one 10-ounce package cooked frozen chopped *spinach* for the broccoli or cauliflower. Drain spinach well, pressing out the excess liquid.

Artichoke- 'n' Mushroom-Topped Pizza: Prepare the Veggie-Topped Pizza as directed above, *except* substitute the artichoke topper for broccoli or cauliflower. For artichoke topper, in a pan combine ½ of a 14-ounce can *artichoke hearts,* cut up, and one 4-ounce can sliced *mushrooms.* Heat through. Drain.

Sweet 'n' Sour Pork

Also try this no-chop stir-fry with frozen Chinese-style vegetables.

½ pound lean boneless pork *or* turkey breast tenderloins
2 tablespoons teriyaki sauce
2 teaspoons cornstarch
1 10-ounce package frozen Japanese-style stir-fry vegetables with seasonings
1 tablespoon cooking oil
1 8-ounce can pineapple tidbits (juice pack)
¼ cup water
   Chow mein noodles

● Thinly slice pork or turkey into bite-size strips, then set aside. Preheat a wok or large skillet over high heat. Meanwhile, for sauce, in a bowl stir together teriyaki sauce and cornstarch. (If frozen vegetables contain a seasoning packet, then stir it into teriyaki mixture.) Set sauce aside.

● Add cooking oil to hot wok or skillet. (If necessary, add more oil during stir-frying.) Add pork or turkey to the wok. Stir-fry over high heat about 3 minutes or till pork is no longer pink or turkey is tender, then remove meat from wok or skillet.

● Add frozen vegetables, *undrained* pineapple, and water to wok. Stir sauce, then add it to wok or skillet. Cook and stir over medium-high heat till thickened and bubbly. Cook and stir for 2 minutes more. Stir in meat and cook about 30 seconds more or till heated through. Serve over chow mein noodles. Serves 3.

Veggie-Topped Pizza
(broccoli version)

Spinach-Topped Pizza

Cranberry-Apple Chops

Serve a stuffing or rice pilaf with these fruity chops, and you've got a complete meal.

1 tablespoon cooking oil
2 pork loin chops *or* smoked
    pork loin chops, cut ½
    inch thick (about 12
    ounces total), *or* one
    8-ounce fully cooked
    boneless ham slice,
    cut about ½ inch thick
  Salt
  Pepper
1 medium apple
¾ cup cranberry-apple drink,
    apple juice, *or* apple cider
2 teaspoons cornstarch
¼ teaspoon ground cinnamon
  Dash ground nutmeg
1 tablespoon butter *or*
    margarine

● Preheat a large skillet over medium-high heat. Add oil. Sprinkle chops with salt and pepper. (For smoked chops or ham, omit oil, salt, and pepper.) Add chops to skillet, then reduce heat to medium. Cook for 7 minutes. Turn chops over. Continue cooking for 5 to 8 minutes more or till no pink remains. (For smoked chops or ham, cook 6 to 10 minutes total, turning once.)

● While meat is cooking, remove core from apple. Cut apple into thin wedges, then set aside. Combine cranberry-apple drink, apple juice, or apple cider; cornstarch; cinnamon; and nutmeg. Set juice mixture aside.

● Transfer meat to a platter and cover. Drain fat from skillet.

● For sauce, in the same skillet melt the butter or margarine. Add apples and cook over medium-high heat about 2 minutes or till nearly tender, stirring occasionally. Stir juice mixture, then add the mixture to the apples in the skillet. Cook and stir over medium-high heat till thickened and bubbly. Cook and stir for 2 minutes more. Serve over meat. Makes 2 servings.

Ham Jubilee

Test Kitchen tip: To hurry up cooking, start cooking the ham on medium-high heat. When the skillet is hot, lower the heat to medium so the ham won't get too brown.

1 8-ounce fully cooked
    boneless ham slice,
    cut about ½ inch thick
1 tablespoon brown sugar
2 teaspoons cornstarch
1 8¾-ounce can pitted dark
    or light sweet cherries
2 tablespoons brandy

● In a large skillet cook ham over medium heat for 3 minutes. Turn ham over, then continue cooking for 3 to 7 minutes more or till heated through. Transfer meat to a serving platter. Cover to keep warm. Remove the skillet from the heat.

● For sauce, in the same skillet, combine brown sugar and cornstarch. Then stir in the *undrained* cherries and brandy. Return the skillet to the heat. Cook and stir till mixture comes to boiling, then reduce heat. Simmer, uncovered, for 2 minutes. Serve over meat. Makes 2 or 3 servings.

Chops Jubilee: Prepare Ham Jubilee as above, *except* substitute three ½-inch-thick *pork loin or veal loin chops* (about 18 ounces total) for the ham. Preheat skillet over medium-high heat. Add 1 tablespoon *cooking oil*. Add chops to the skillet. Reduce heat to medium. Cook for 12 to 15 minutes or till pork is no longer pink or till veal is to desired doneness, turning once.
● While chops are cooking, prepare sauce in a small saucepan. Serve as above.

Broccoli 'n' Turkey Roll-Ups

Cheese spread + milk = a super-simple sauce.

1 **10-ounce package frozen broccoli *or* asparagus spears**

8 **ounces thinly sliced, fully cooked turkey breast *or* ham**

2 **English muffins**

1 **5-ounce jar cheese spread with blue cheese *or* ½ of an 8-ounce container port wine- *or* Swiss-flavored cold-pack cheese food**

¼ **cup milk**
   Paprika (optional)

● Place frozen broccoli or asparagus spears in a colander. Run *hot water* over vegetable just till thawed. Drain well. Meanwhile, in a large skillet or an electric skillet place a wire rack or a large open steamer basket. Pour in enough *hot water* to almost reach the rack. Bring to boiling, then reduce to a simmer.

● While water is coming to a boil, for vegetable rolls, divide meat into 4 portions. Place thawed broccoli or asparagus spears on one edge of each meat portion. Roll meat around vegetables. If necessary, secure with wooden toothpicks. Carefully place rolls, seam sides down, on the wire rack or steamer basket. Cover skillet. Steam about 10 minutes or till heated through.

● While vegetable rolls are steaming, split and toast muffins. For sauce, in a saucepan combine cheese and milk. Cook over medium heat till cheese is melted, stirring occasionally.

● To serve, place a vegetable roll on top of each muffin half. If necessary, remove toothpicks. Spoon warm sauce over rolls and muffins. If desired, sprinkle with paprika. Makes 4 servings.

Assembling the roll-ups
Use either sliced luncheon meat or thinly sliced meat from the deli for the meat-vegetable rolls. Divide the meat into 4 portions. Then place some of the broccoli or asparagus spears on one edge of each portion of meat. Roll the meat around the vegetables jelly-roll style. Secure the vegetable rolls with wooden toothpicks.

Carefully place the vegetable rolls, with their seam sides down, on the wire rack or steamer basket. Then cover the skillet and steam the vegetable rolls about 10 minutes or till they are heated through.

Pineapple Turkey

Look for hoisin (HOY-SIN) sauce in the Oriental section of the supermarket.

2 10-ounce packages frozen
   broccoli spears
1 tablespoon butter *or*
   margarine
1 pound turkey breast
   tenderloins *or* boned
   skinless chicken breast
   halves
1 15½-ounce can pineapple
   chunks
2 teaspoons cornstarch
2 teaspoons hoisin sauce
½ teaspoon ground ginger
1 tablespoon diced pimiento

● Cook frozen broccoli according to package directions, then drain. If necessary, cover to keep warm.

● While broccoli is cooking, in a large skillet melt butter or margarine. Meanwhile, slice poultry into ¾-inch-wide strips. Then add it to the skillet. Cook over medium-high heat about 4 minutes or *just* till tender, turning pieces over occasionally.

● While poultry is cooking, for the sauce, in a bowl stir together *undrained* pineapple, cornstarch, hoisin sauce, and ginger.

● Push poultry to sides of skillet. Then add sauce to center. Cook and stir till thickened and bubbly. Cook and stir over medium heat for 1 minute more. Add the pimiento and toss mixture lightly to coat with sauce.

● To serve, arrange broccoli on a serving platter. Spoon poultry mixture on top. Makes 4 servings.

Broiled Chicken Cordon Bleu

So elegant, it's hard to believe this dish takes less than 15 minutes to make. (Pictured opposite and on the cover.)

2 boned skinless chicken
   breast halves *or* turkey
   breast tenderloins
   (about 8 ounces total)
1 tablespoon soft *or* whipped
   margarine
2 slices process Swiss
   cheese (2 ounces)
   Coarse-grain brown
   mustard *or* Dijon-style
   mustard
2 thin slices fully cooked ham
   or Canadian-style bacon
   Paprika
   Cherry tomatoes (optional)
   Parsley sprigs (optional)

● Preheat broiler. Meanwhile, place poultry on the unheated rack of the broiler pan. Brush with *half* of the margarine.

● Broil 4 inches from the heat for 4 minutes. Turn poultry over and brush with remaining margarine. Broil for 4 to 5 minutes more or till tender. Meanwhile, cut cheese slices in half.

● Brush tops of poultry with mustard. Place one-half slice of cheese on top of each piece of poultry, then top with the ham or bacon. (If necessary, cut ham slice to fit poultry.) Broil about 30 seconds or till ham is warm. Then top with remaining cheese. Broil for ½ to 1 minute more or till cheese is melted.

● To serve, transfer to dinner plates. Sprinkle with paprika. If desired, garnish with tomatoes and parsley. Makes 2 servings.

To micro-cook: Omit margarine. Cook poultry in microwave oven according to tip directions on page 24. Drain. Cut cheese as above. Brush poultry with mustard. Top with *half* of the cheese, ham, then remaining cheese. Cook, covered, on high about 30 seconds more or just till cheese melts. Serve as above.

Broiled Chicken
Cordon Bleu

Choose-a-Sauce Poultry

Either pan-fry or micro-cook the poultry, then add one of our four toppers. (Orange-Hoisin Sauced Poultry is pictured on page 9.)

2 **tablespoons butter** *or*
    margarine
4 **boned skinless chicken**
    breast halves *or* **turkey**
    breast tenderloins (about
    1 pound total)

● In a large skillet melt butter or margarine. Add the chicken or turkey. Cook over medium heat for 8 to 10 minutes or till tender, turning the pieces over occasionally to brown evenly. Transfer the chicken or turkey to a serving platter.

● While poultry is cooking, prepare the glaze or one of the sauces below. Brush on or serve over poultry. Makes 4 servings.

Honey-Curry Glaze: In a small bowl stir together 1 tablespoon *Dijon-style mustard,* 1 tablespoon *honey,* ½ teaspoon *lemon juice,* and ¼ teaspoon *curry powder.* During the last 2 minutes of pan-frying, brush honey mixture over poultry.

Orange Sauce: In a small saucepan combine ¾ cup *orange juice* and 2 tablespoons *cornstarch.* Cook and stir till thickened and bubbly. Cook and stir for 2 minutes more. Meanwhile, drain one 11-ounce can *mandarin orange sections,* then stir sections into sauce. *Or,* stir in ¼ cup sliced *almonds.*

Orange-Hoisin Sauce: In a saucepan combine ⅓ cup *orange marmalade,* 2 teaspoons *hoisin sauce,* and ½ teaspoon ground *ginger.* Cook and stir till heated through.

Mustard-Caper Sauce: In a small saucepan combine ½ cup *milk* and 2 teaspoons *all-purpose flour.* Stir in 1 tablespoon *Dijon-style mustard* and 1 tablespoon drained *capers.* Cook and stir till thickened and bubbly. Cook and stir for 1 minute more.

Micro-Cooking Chicken and Turkey

With a touch of a button, your microwave oven can cook poultry in minutes.

Place boned skinless chicken breast halves in a 10x6x2-inch baking dish or place turkey breast tenderloins in a 12x7½x2-inch baking dish.

Cover with vented microwave-safe plastic wrap. Micro-cook on 100% power (high) for 1½ minutes for 8 ounces of poultry; 3 minutes for 1 pound. Rearrange and turn poultry pieces over (move outside pieces to center of dish). Then cook, covered, on high for ½ to 1½ minutes more for 8 ounces, 3 to 4 minutes more for 1 pound, or till tender.

Chicken Cacciatore

4 ounces medium noodles
2 tablespoons butter *or*
   margarine
1 pound boned skinless
   chicken breast halves
   or turkey breast
   tenderloins
1 2½-ounce jar sliced
   mushrooms
1 15½-ounce jar chunky-style
   meatless spaghetti sauce
½ cup frozen chopped green
   pepper (see tip, page 12)
¼ cup dry red wine
   Grated *or* finely shredded
   Parmesan cheese
   (optional)

● Cook pasta according to the package directions, *except* use a 3-quart saucepan and 4 cups *hot* water. Then drain.

● While pasta is cooking, in a large skillet melt butter or margarine. Meanwhile, slice each chicken or turkey piece lengthwise into 3 pieces. Then add poultry to the skillet. Cook over medium heat for 6 to 8 minutes or till tender, turning pieces over once.

● While poultry is cooking, drain mushrooms. For sauce, stir together mushrooms, spaghetti sauce, frozen green pepper, and wine. Add it to poultry in skillet. Cook and stir occasionally over medium-high heat or till heated through. Serve over hot pasta. If desired, sprinkle with the Parmesan cheese. Serves 4.

To micro-cook: Cook pasta and cut up poultry as above. Omit butter. Micro-cook the poultry in a 12x7½x2-inch baking dish according to tip directions opposite. Drain off liquid.
● For sauce, in a 1-quart microwave-safe casserole stir together the sauce ingredients as above, *except* omit the poultry. Micro-cook, uncovered, on 100% power (high) about 4 minutes or till bubbly, stirring once. Toss sauce with poultry. Serve as above.

Oriental Gingered Turkey with Cashews

   Chow mein noodles *or* 1 cup
   quick-cooking rice
8 ounces turkey breast
   tenderloins *or* boned
   skinless chicken breast
   halves
1 small carrot
1 cup orange juice
¼ cup soy sauce
½ to 1 teaspoon ground ginger
   Dash ground red pepper
1 tablespoon cooking oil
1 10-ounce package frozen
   cauliflower
1 tablespoon cornstarch
½ cup unsalted cashews
   or walnut halves

● If serving rice, cook it according to package directions.

● While rice is cooking, slice the turkey or chicken into bite-size strips, then set aside. Thinly bias-slice carrot, then set aside. Preheat a wok or large skillet over high heat. Meanwhile, for sauce, in a small mixing bowl stir together ½ *cup* of the orange juice, soy sauce, ginger, and red pepper. Set sauce aside.

● Add cooking oil to hot wok or skillet. (If necessary, add more cooking oil during stir-frying.) Add turkey or chicken and carrot to the wok or skillet. Stir-fry over high heat about 3 minutes or till poultry is tender, then remove from wok or skillet.

● Add sauce and frozen cauliflower to wok or skillet. Bring mixture to boiling, then reduce heat. Cover and simmer for 2 minutes. Meanwhile, combine remaining juice and cornstarch. Stir juice-cornstarch mixture into mixture in wok. Cook and stir over medium-high heat till thickened and bubbly. Cook and stir for 2 minutes more. Stir in the poultry-carrot mixture and cashews or walnuts. Cook just till heat through. Serve over chow mein noodles or the hot rice. Makes 3 servings.

Lemony Oriental-Style Chicken Chunks

1 12-ounce package frozen, breaded, small, chunk-shape chicken patties
3 green onions
¼ of a medium head iceberg lettuce
1 cup water
¼ cup lemon juice
3 tablespoons brown sugar
2 tablespoons soy sauce
4 teaspoons cornstarch
½ teaspoon instant chicken bouillon granules
1 tablespoon cooking oil

● Preheat oven, then bake the chicken according to package directions. Meanwhile, bias-slice the green onions into 1-inch pieces and shred the lettuce.

● While chicken is baking, preheat wok or large skillet over high heat. In a bowl stir together water, lemon juice, sugar, soy sauce, cornstarch, and bouillon granules. Set sauce aside.

● Add oil to the hot wok. Add onions. Stir-fry for 1 minute. Push onions from center. Stir sauce, then add it to wok. Cook and stir till thickened and bubbly. Cook and stir for 2 minutes more. Add chicken. Toss to coat. Serve over lettuce. Serves 4.

To micro-cook: Cook chicken in the microwave oven according to package directions. Cover to keep warm. Meanwhile, bias-slice onions into 1-inch pieces and shred lettuce.
● For sauce, in a 4-cup measure combine sugar and cornstarch. Stir in onions, water, juice, soy sauce, and bouillon granules. Omit oil. Micro-cook, uncovered, on 100% power (high) 4 to 6 minutes or till thickened and bubbly, stirring after every minute. Add to chicken. Toss. Serve as above.

Shredding lettuce
Whether you're shredding iceberg lettuce for the Lemony Oriental-Style Chicken Chunks or for a salad, here's how to do it quickly.

First cut the head into quarters. Then, holding a quarter-head firmly against a cutting board, use a long-bladed knife to cut the lettuce into long, coarse ¼-inch-wide shreds. You should have about 3 cups of shredded lettuce from a quarter-head of lettuce.

Plantation Shortcake

It's a cheesy southern-style chicken 'n' ham sauce over corn bread.

1 slice fully cooked ham
(about 1 ounce)
1 2½-ounce jar sliced
mushrooms
1 slice process Swiss cheese
(1 ounce)
2 tablespoons butter *or*
margarine
2 tablespoons all-purpose
flour
½ teaspoon instant chicken
bouillon granules
Dash pepper
1 cup milk
1 cup frozen diced cooked
chicken
2 corn bread squares *or*
muffins, English muffins,
or baking powder biscuits
Fresh parsley (optional)

● For sauce, finely chop ham, drain mushrooms, and tear cheese slice into pieces, then set aside. In a medium saucepan melt butter or margarine. Stir in the flour, bouillon granules, and pepper. Add milk. Cook and stir over medium-high heat till thickened and bubbly. Stir in cheese till melted. Then stir in ham, mushrooms, and frozen chicken, and heat through.

● While sauce is cooking, if serving English muffins, split and toast them.

● To serve, spoon sauce over the corn bread, English muffins, or biscuits. If desired, snip parsley on top. Makes 2 servings.

To micro-cook: Prepare ham, mushrooms, and cheese for sauce as above. In a 1-quart microwave-safe casserole place butter or margarine. Micro-cook, uncovered, on 100% power (high) for 45 to 60 seconds or till melted. Stir in flour, bouillon granules, and pepper. Add milk. Cook, uncovered, on high for 3 to 5 minutes or till thickened, stirring after every minute.
● Stir in ham, mushrooms, cheese, and frozen chicken. Then cook, uncovered, on high for 2 to 4 minutes more or till cheese is melted and mixture is heated through, stirring once or twice. Serve as above.

Chicken Divan

Measuring takes time. So start with a white sauce mix as the base for this chicken-Dijon sauce. The mix has the ingredients already measured out for you.

2 10-ounce packages frozen
broccoli spears
1 1¾-ounce envelope white
sauce mix
1 12-ounce package frozen
diced cooked chicken
(3 cups)
2 tablespoons Dijon-style
mustard
2 teaspoons instant chicken
bouillon granules
½ cup plain croutons *or* ¼ cup
sliced almonds
Paprika (optional)

● Cook broccoli according to package directions. Then drain.

● While broccoli is cooking, prepare white sauce mix according to package directions, *except* stir in frozen chicken, mustard, and bouillon granules before cooking.

● To serve, arrange broccoli in a deep serving platter. Spoon chicken mixture over broccoli. Top with croutons or almonds. If desired, sprinkle with paprika. Makes 4 servings.

Sour-Cream-Topped
Fish Platter

Shanghai Dinner

Leftover beef or pork is also great in this Oriental one-dish meal.

1 11-ounce can fried rice
¼ cup water
1 tablespoon dry sherry
½ teaspoon ground ginger
1 6-ounce package frozen pea pods
8 ounces sliced fully cooked turkey breast

● In a medium saucepan combine rice, water, sherry, and ginger, then cover. Cook over medium heat about 5 minutes or till heated through, stirring occasionally.

● While rice mixture is cooking, place frozen pea pods in a colander. Run *hot water* over pea pods just till thawed. Drain well, then set aside. Cut turkey into bite-size julienne strips.

● Stir pea pods and turkey into rice mixture. Cover and cook over low heat about 5 minutes more or till heated through. Makes 4 servings.

To micro-cook: Place rice, water, sherry, and ginger in a 1½-quart microwave-safe casserole, then cover. Micro-cook on 100% power (high) for 2 to 3 minutes or till heated through, stirring once.
● Meanwhile, thaw pea pods and cut up turkey as above. Stir them into the rice mixture. Cook, covered, on high for 3 to 4 minutes more or till heated through, stirring once.

Sour-Cream-Topped Fish Platter

Pompano is mild in flavor; sole, flounder, and orange roughy have a delicate flavor.

1 10-ounce package frozen Chinese- *or* Japanese-style stir-fry vegetables with seasonings
12 ounces skinless pompano, flounder, orange roughy, *or* sole fillets (about ½ inch thick)
¼ cup dairy sour cream
1 tablespoon all-purpose flour
¼ teaspoon dried basil, crushed

● In a 10-inch covered skillet combine ½ cup *hot water*, frozen vegetables, and seasonings from packet in frozen vegetables. Bring just to boiling. If necessary, use a fork to break vegetables apart. Then carefully place fish on top of vegetables. Return just to boiling, then reduce the heat. Cover and simmer gently for 4 to 6 minutes or till fish flakes easily with a fork and vegetables are tender.

● While fish is cooking, in a small mixing bowl stir together sour cream, flour, and basil. Set sour cream mixture aside.

● When fish and vegetables are done, use a slotted spatula to transfer the fish to a serving platter. Then drain vegetables, reserving ⅓ *cup* of the liquid. Arrange the vegetables on the platter. Cover to keep warm.

● For sauce, stir reserved liquid into sour cream mixture. Then transfer mixture to the skillet. Cook and stir over medium heat till thickened and bubbly. Cook and stir for 1 minute more. Make 3 servings.

Poached Salmon with Cucumber Sauce

Need a cool meal on a hot summer day? Cook these steaks up to two days ahead, then chill them and serve the chilled fish with the refreshing cucumber sauce.

2 cups water *or* 1½ cups water *plus* ½ cup dry white wine
1 bay leaf
4 salmon, cod, halibut, *or* shark steaks, cut 1 inch thick (about 2 pounds total)
¼ of a small cucumber
⅓ cup plain yogurt
1 teaspoon frozen snipped chives
¼ teaspoon sugar

● In a large skillet combine water or water plus wine, and bay leaf. Bring just to boiling. Carefully add the fish. Return just to boiling, then reduce the heat. Cover and simmer gently for 8 to 12 minutes or till fish flakes easily with a fork.

● While fish is cooking, prepare the cucumber sauce. Shred the cucumber (you should have about 3 tablespoons). In a small mixing bowl stir together the shredded cucumber, yogurt, chives, and sugar.

● To serve immediately, use a slotted spatula to transfer fish to a serving platter. Spoon sauce over warm fish. Serves 4.

To micro-cook: Omit water, wine, and bay leaf. To cook fish, place it in a single layer in a greased 12x7½x2-inch baking dish. Brush fish lightly with *cooking oil.* Cover with vented microwave-safe plastic wrap. Micro-cook on 100% power (high) for 4 minutes. Rearrange and turn steaks over (move outside steaks to the center of dish). Cook, covered, on high for 2 to 4 minutes more or till fish flakes easily with a fork. Meanwhile, prepare sauce as above. Serve as above.

Tomato- 'n' Zucchini-Topped Halibut

To micro-cook the fish, use the directions above for Poached Salmon with Cucumber Sauce.

4 halibut *or* swordfish steaks, cut 1 inch thick (about 2 pounds total)
1 2½-ounce jar sliced mushrooms
1 16-ounce can zucchini in Italian-style tomato sauce
¼ cup frozen chopped green pepper (see tip, page 12)
½ teaspoon Italian seasoning

● Pour about ½-inch *hot water* into a large skillet. Bring water just to boiling. Carefully add the fish. Return just to boiling, then reduce the heat. Cover and simmer gently for 8 to 12 minutes or till fish flakes easily with a fork.

● While fish is cooking, prepare sauce. Drain mushrooms. In a medium saucepan combine the mushrooms, zucchini in tomato sauce, frozen green pepper, and Italian seasoning. Bring to boiling, then reduce heat. Cover and simmer for 3 minutes.

● To serve, use a slotted spatula to transfer fish to dinner plates. Spoon sauce over fish. Serve immediately. Makes 4 servings.

Crumb-Topped Fish Steaks

Fish—it's so easy to cook. And you'll see why when you try this corn-breaded fish recipe.

4 halibut, salmon, *or* sea bass steaks, *or* skinless cod fillets (¾ to 1 inch thick) (about 1½ pounds total)
1 tablespoon cooking oil
2 tablespoons butter *or* margarine
⅓ cup corn bread stuffing mix
2 tablespoons frozen snipped chives
¼ teaspoon onion powder
⅛ teaspoon pepper

● Preheat broiler. Meanwhile, if using cod fillets, cut them into 4 serving-size portions. Place the fish on a greased rack of an unheated broiler pan, tucking under any thin edges. Brush fish with the cooking oil.

● Broil fish 4 inches from heat for 6 to 12 minutes or till fish flakes easily with a fork. Meanwhile, for the crumb mixture, in a small saucepan melt butter or margarine. Stir in stuffing mix, chives, onion powder, and pepper. Then remove from heat.

● Top cooked fish with crumb mixture. Broil fish about 30 seconds more or till crumbs are slightly toasted. Serves 4.

Lemon-Dill Haddock

Brush on the flavor. The buttery sauce pleasantly accents the delicate flavor of haddock.

1 pound skinless haddock, cod, *or* orange roughy fillets (½ to ¾ inch thick)
1 tablespoon butter *or* margarine
2 tablespoons lemon juice
½ teaspoon dried dillweed
¼ teaspoon garlic salt

● Preheat broiler. Meanwhile, place fish on a greased rack of an unheated broiler pan, tucking under any thin edges. Then set aside. In a small saucepan melt the butter or margarine. Stir in lemon juice, dill, and garlic salt. Brush fish with butter mixture.

● Broil fish 4 inches from the heat for 4 to 9 minutes or till fish flakes easily with a fork. Makes 4 servings.

Fishing for Substitutions?

Unsure of which fish you like? Here's a quick flavor and texture guide to help you decide:
● *Cod, flounder, haddock, halibut, orange roughy, sea bass,* and *sole* are popular because of their *very* delicate flavor.
● *Grouper, pike, pollack, pompano,* and *red snapper* are mild in flavor and flaky in texture.
● *Shark* and *swordfish* are also mild in flavor but have a firm, dense texture.
● *Catfish* can take on the flavor of the water it's grown in. Farm-raised catfish has a delicate flavor, whereas lake catfish has a slightly richer flavor.
● *Monkfish* is sometimes called "poor man's lobster." It has a sweet flavor and firm, dense texture that is similar to lobster, but it usually costs less.

20-Minute Paella

20-Minute Paella

Frozen, shelled cooked shrimp work well, too. Just remember—place them in the refrigerator the night before to thaw.

1 cup frozen diced cooked chicken
½ cup long grain rice
¼ cup frozen peas
¼ cup frozen chopped onion (see tip, page 12)
1 teaspoon instant chicken bouillon granules
¼ teaspoon bottle minced garlic *or* dash of garlic powder
⅛ teaspoon ground saffron *or* ground turmeric
  Dash ground red pepper
6 ounces shrimp cooked in shells
½ of a 7¾-ounce can artichoke hearts
1 tablespoon diced pimiento

● In a medium saucepan combine 1 cup *hot water,* frozen chicken, rice, frozen peas, frozen onion, bouillon granules, garlic, saffron or turmeric, and red pepper. Bring to boiling, then reduce heat. Cover and cook over low heat for 13 minutes.

● While rice mixture is cooking, remove shells from shrimp. If artichoke hearts are marinated, drain and rinse them. Then stir the shrimp, artichokes, and pimiento into the cooked rice mixture. Cover and cook for 1 to 2 minutes more or till shrimp are heated through. Makes 2 servings.

Seafood Primavera

1 5-ounce package corkscrew macaroni with vegetables and cream sauce *or* one 4½-ounce package noodles with Parmesan cheese sauce
1½ cups loose-pack frozen mixed zucchini, carrots, cauliflower, lima beans, and Italian beans, *or* frozen mixed cauliflower, broccoli, and carrots
½ teaspoon dried basil, crushed
1 8-ounce package frozen peeled and deveined shrimp *or* 8 ounces crab-flavored fish sticks
1 3-ounce package cream cheese
1 medium tomato

● Cook pasta mix according to package directions, *except* add frozen mixed vegetables and basil to the boiling water with the pasta mix. If using frozen shrimp, add them to mixture the last 2 minutes of cooking.

● While pasta mix is cooking, if using crab-flavored fish sticks, cut them into 1-inch pieces. Cut cream cheese into cubes. Cut tomato into wedges.

● If using fish sticks, add pieces to pasta mixture. Then add cream cheese to the pasta mixture. Cook, covered, over low heat about 2 minutes more or till cream cheese is melted and fish is heated through.

● To serve, spoon mixture onto dinner plates and garnish with tomato wedges. Makes 3 servings.

Crab Enchiladas

Turn your skillet into an on-top-of-the-range oven to heat the enchiladas.

½ of an 8-ounce container soft-
　style cream cheese with
　chives and onion
½ cup shredded Monterey
　Jack cheese (2 ounces)
1 tablespoon milk
1 6-ounce can crabmeat
4 6-inch flour tortillas
¾ cup mild salsa

● For filling, in a small saucepan combine the cream cheese, Monterey Jack cheese, and milk. Cook over medium-high heat for 4 to 5 minutes or till cheeses are melted, stirring often. Meanwhile, drain, flake, and remove the cartilage from crab. Then stir the crab into the cheese mixture. Continue cooking and stirring occasionally just till heated through.

● To assemble enchiladas, spoon filling down center of each tortilla and roll up. Place enchiladas, seam side down, in a large skillet. Cover. Cook over medium heat for 3 to 5 minutes or till heated through. Meanwhile, in a small saucepan heat salsa.

● To serve, transfer enchiladas to dinner plates. Spoon warm salsa over enchiladas. Makes 2 servings.

To micro-cook: Stir crab filling together as above, *except* do not heat filling. Assemble enchiladas. Then place the enchiladas in a 10x6x2-inch baking dish. Cover with vented microwave-safe plastic wrap. Micro-cook on 100% power (high) for 3 minutes. Turn dish a quarter-turn. Cook, covered, on high for 2 to 3 minutes more or till heated through. Keep covered.
● Transfer salsa to a 2-cup measure. Cook, uncovered, on high about 1 minute or till heated through. Serve as above.

Shrimp Étouffée

Étouffée (AY-too-FAY) is a spicy seafood sauce. To use fresh shrimp in this Cajun dish, cook them separately, then stir them in at the end.

1½ cups frozen chopped onion
　　(see tip, page 12)
1 cup frozen chopped green
　pepper (see tip, page 12)
1 teaspoon bottle minced
　garlic *or* ¼ teaspoon garlic
　powder
¼ teaspoon celery seed
¼ cup butter *or* margarine
1½ cups quick-cooking rice
2 tablespoons cornstarch
¼ teaspoon ground red pepper
¼ teaspoon black pepper
1 8-ounce can tomato sauce
2 8-ounce packages frozen
　cooked shrimp

● In a large skillet cook frozen onion, green pepper, garlic, and celery seed in butter or margarine over medium-high heat about 5 minutes or till the vegetables are tender but not brown, stirring occasionally.

● While vegetables are cooking, cook rice according to package directions. For sauce, combine cornstarch, red pepper, black pepper, ¼ cup *water,* and ½ teaspoon *salt.*

● Stir the cornstarch mixture and tomato sauce into the cooked vegetables. Then stir in the frozen shrimp. Bring to boiling, then reduce heat. Cover and simmer about 3 minutes or just till the shrimp are heated through.

● To serve, spoon sauce and shrimp over the hot cooked rice. Makes 4 servings.

Surf 'n' Turf Kabobs

Dining alone? This recipe easily cuts in half.

2 tablespoons butter *or* margarine

⅛ teaspoon garlic powder

⅛ teaspoon dried dillweed

4 ounces beef tenderloin *or* boneless beef sirloin steak, cut 1 inch thick

4 ounces shelled shrimp

8 whole fresh mushrooms

¾ cup quick-cooking rice *or* ½ cup quick-cooking couscous (optional)

Salt

Pepper

● Preheat broiler. Meanwhile, in a small saucepan combine butter or margarine, garlic powder, and dillweed. Heat over low heat till butter or margarine is melted.

● While butter is melting, assemble kabobs. Slice beef across the grain into ¼-inch-thick strips. Using 4 medium skewers, alternately thread beef, shrimp, and mushrooms, leaving about a ¼-inch space between pieces. Place on the unheated rack of the broiler pan. Brush kabobs with some of the butter mixture.

● Broil kabobs 3 inches from heat for 4 minutes. Turn kabobs over. Brush with more butter mixture. Broil about 4 minutes more or till shrimp turn pink and steak is to desired doneness.

● If desired, while the kabobs are broiling, cook rice or couscous according to package directions. Serve hot rice or couscous with kabobs. Season kabobs to taste with salt and pepper. Serves 2.

Assembling the kabobs
To assemble the kabobs, thread the beef onto the skewers in a slightly open accordion-fashion. Then alternate it with the shrimp and mushrooms, leaving about ¼ inch of space between the pieces. The space allows the the food to cook faster and more evenly.

35

Swiss-Sauced Tortellini with Asparagus

There is a difference—fresh and frozen tortellini cook faster than dried.

1 **7-ounce package cheese-filled tortellini (not dried)**
1 **8-** *or* **10-ounce package frozen cut asparagus**
1 **4-ounce can sliced mushrooms**
1 **2-ounce jar diced pimiento**
4 **ounces sliced process Swiss cheese**
2 **tablespoons butter** *or* **margarine**
2 **tablespoons all-purpose flour**
⅛ **teaspoon ground nutmeg**
1 **cup milk**

● Cook tortellini according to package directions, *except* use a 3-quart saucepan, 4 cups *hot* water, and add frozen asparagus the last 3 to 5 minutes of cooking. Then drain.

● While tortellini and asparagus are cooking, prepare sauce. Drain mushrooms and pimiento. Tear cheese slices into pieces, then set aside. In a medium saucepan melt butter or margarine. Stir in flour and nutmeg. Add milk. Cook and stir over medium-high heat till thickened and bubbly. Cook and stir for 1 minute more. Then add mushrooms, pimiento, and Swiss cheese. Cook and stir just till cheese is melted.

● To serve, pour cheese sauce over hot tortellini and asparagus. Toss lightly to coat. Transfer to a serving dish. Serves 4.

To micro-cook: Cook tortellini and asparagus as above. For sauce, in a medium microwave-safe bowl place butter or margarine. Micro-cook, uncovered, on 100% power (high) for 45 to 60 seconds or till melted. Stir in flour and nutmeg. Add milk. Cook, uncovered, on high for 3 to 5 minutes or till thickened, stirring after every minute. Stir in drained mushrooms, pimiento, and torn cheese. Cook, uncovered, on high for 1 to 1½ minutes more or till cheese is melted, stirring once. Serve as above.

Mexican Egg Roll-Ups

4 **7-inch flour tortillas**
2 **tablespoons butter** *or* **margarine**
4 **eggs**
⅓ **cup milk** *or* **light cream**
⅛ **teaspoon salt**
½ **cup shredded Monterey Jack cheese (2 ounces)**
½ **cup shredded cheddar cheese (2 ounces)**
   Green onion (optional)
   Dairy sour cream
   Hot salsa
   Shredded Monterey Jack *or* **cheddar cheese (optional)**

● If desired, warm the tortillas according to the tip directions on page 56. Meanwhile, in a large skillet melt butter or margarine.

● While butter is melting, use a fork to beat eggs, milk or cream, and salt till well combined. Pour mixture into the skillet. Cook over medium heat, without stirring, till mixture begins to set on bottom and edges. Then using a large spatula, lift and fold partially cooked eggs so the uncooked portions flow underneath. Cook about 3 minutes more or till eggs are cooked throughout but are still glossy and moist. Then sprinkle with ½ cup Monterey Jack and ½ cup cheddar cheese. Remove from heat. Cover. Let stand about 1 minute or till cheese melts.

● While cheese is melting, if using green onion, slice it. To serve, spoon some of the egg mixture at one edge of each tortilla. Top with sour cream, then drizzle with salsa. Roll tortillas around mixture. Place rolls-ups on dinner plates. If desired, top with onion or additional sour cream, salsa, or cheese. Serves 4.

SUPPERTIME SOUPS AND STEWS

20 MIN

Whoever said a "good" soup or stew has to simmer a long time? Not us. We've streamlined our soups and stews so that you can prepare homemade soups, stews, gumbos, and chowders in just minutes without any fuss.

Making a Quick Switch

Oops! You're out of an ingredient. No need to fret—check the list below for some emergency substitutions:

Ingredient	Substitution
1 tablespoon cornstarch	2 tablespoons all-purpose flour (for thickening)
1 teaspoon baking powder	1 teaspoon baking soda *plus* ½ cup buttermilk *or* sour milk (to replace the ½ cup liquid called for)
1 cup whole milk	½ cup evaporated milk *plus* ½ cup water, *or* 1 cup reconstituted nonfat dry milk
1 cup light cream	2 tablespoons butter *plus* 1 cup *minus* 2 tablespoons milk
2 cups tomato sauce	¾ cup tomato paste *plus* 1 cup water
1 cup tomato juice	½ cup tomato sauce *plus* ½ cup water
½ teaspoon bottled minced garlic	⅛ teaspoon garlic powder *or* 1 clove garlic
1 small onion (⅓ cup chopped)	1 teaspoon onion powder *or* 1 tablespoon dried minced onion
1 tablespoon prepared mustard	1 teaspoon dry mustard
1 teaspoon dried herbs, crushed	1 tablespoon snipped fresh herbs

Toppers for Pizzazz

Dress up soups with these quick-as-a-wink ideas:

Use any kind of shredded or grated cheese, purchased bacon pieces, sour cream, yogurt, croutons, nuts, popcorn, crushed crackers, chow mein noodles, fresh herbs and parsley, sliced green onion or avocado, chopped hard-cooked eggs (see tip, page 56) or dill pickles, shredded carrot or zucchini, sliced cucumber or olives, and any kind of sprouts.

Chili Con Carne

For a complete cold-weather meal, top this zesty chili with sour cream or cheese and serve it with corn bread or crackers.

½ pound ground beef *or*
    ground raw turkey
¼ cup frozen chopped onion
    (see tip, page 12)
2 to 3 teaspoons chili powder
1 7½-ounce can tomatoes
1 8-ounce can red kidney
    beans
½ teaspoon bottled minced
    garlic *or* ⅛ teaspoon garlic
    powder
    Several dashes bottled hot
    pepper sauce

● Break ground meat into large pieces while adding it to a medium skillet. Cook meat, frozen onion, and chili powder over high heat till the beef is brown or turkey is no longer pink and onion is tender. Drain off fat. Meanwhile, cut up tomatoes.

● Stir *undrained* tomatoes, *undrained* kidney beans, garlic, and pepper sauce into meat mixture. Bring to boiling, then reduce the heat. Simmer, uncovered, for 5 minutes, stirring occasionally. Makes 2 servings.

To micro-cook: Place the loose ground meat, onion, and chili powder in a 1½-quart microwave-safe casserole, then cover. Micro-cook on 100% (high) for 3½ to 5 minutes or till meat is no longer pink, stirring once. Drain off fat. Cut up tomatoes.
● Stir in the *undrained* tomatoes, *undrained* kidney beans, garlic, and pepper sauce. Then cook, uncovered, on high for 2 to 4 minutes or till heated through, stirring once.

Quick Old-Fashioned Tomato-Beef Stew

Two for one: Cook a large roast for dinner on Sunday and save enough meat for stew during the week. (Pictured on page 41.)

1 29-ounce can large-cut
    mixed vegetables
12 ounces cooked boneless
    beef
1 16-ounce can tomatoes
3 tablespoons cornstarch
1 10½-ounce can condensed
    beef broth
¾ cup hot water
½ cup frozen chopped onion
    (see tip, page 12)
½ teaspoon dried thyme,
    crushed
½ teaspoon bottled minced
    garlic *or* ⅛ teaspoon garlic
    powder
¼ teaspoon pepper
    Corn bread squares,
    muffins, *or* baking powder
    biscuits (optional)

● Drain the mixed vegetables. Cut beef into ½-inch cubes (you should have about 2 cups). Set vegetables and beef aside.

● Cut up tomatoes. In a large saucepan combine the *undrained* tomatoes and cornstarch. Then stir in beef broth, hot water, frozen onion, thyme, garlic, and pepper. Cook and stir over medium-high heat till thickened and bubbly.

● Add the drained vegetables and cubed beef to the tomato mixture. Cook for 2 to 3 minutes more or till heated through. If desired, serve with corn bread, muffins, or biscuits. Serves 6.

Add-On Potato Soup

Combine the new with the old. Cucumber and ham are the add-ons to a quick, old-fashioned potato soup.

12 ounces fully cooked
    boneless ham
½ of a small cucumber
2 cups milk
1 teaspoon instant chicken
    bouillon granules
½ cup dairy sour cream *or*
    plain yogurt
1 tablespoon all-purpose flour
1 cup frozen hash brown
    potatoes with onion and
    peppers
    Frozen snipped chives

● Cut ham into ½-inch cubes (you should have about 2 cups). Seed and chop cucumber (you should have about ½ cup).

● In a large saucepan combine ham, cucumber, milk, and bouillon granules. Bring mixture just to boiling. Meanwhile, stir together sour cream or yogurt and flour.

● Stir frozen potatoes into ham mixture. Then stir in the sour cream or yogurt mixture. Cook over medium-high heat until heated through, stirring occasionally. *Do not boil.* Top with chives to serve. Makes 4 servings.

To micro-cook: Prepare ham and cucumber as above. In a 2-quart microwave-safe casserole combine ham, cucumber, milk, and bouillon granules. Micro-cook, uncovered, on 100% power (high) for 7 to 8 minutes or till milk is heated through, stirring twice. Meanwhile, stir together sour cream or yogurt and flour.
● Stir potatoes and sour cream mixture into ham mixture. Cook, uncovered, on high about 3 to 4 minutes or till heated through, stirring after every minute. *Do not boil.* Serve as above.

Hearty Noodle Stew

Italian seasonings give this delicious stew an ethnic twist.

1 14½-ounce can tomatoes
1¾ cup hot water
1 9-ounce package frozen
    Italian green beans
½ cup frozen chopped onion
    (see tip, page 12)
1 3-ounce package Oriental
    noodles with chicken
    flavor
1 teaspoon dried oregano,
    crushed
1 teaspoon dried marjoram,
    crushed
1 16-ounce fully cooked
    smoked turkey sausage
    link
    Grated *or* finely shredded
    Parmesan cheese
    (optional)

● Cut up tomatoes. In a large saucepan combine *undrained* tomatoes, hot water, frozen beans, frozen onion, seasoning packet from the Oriental noodles, oregano, and marjoram. Bring to boiling.

● While tomato mixture is coming to a boil, cut sausage link lengthwise in half. Then cut halves into 1-inch pieces.

● When tomato mixture comes to a boil, slightly break up the noodles while adding them to the tomato mixture. Then add sausage. Return mixture to boiling, then reduce heat. Cover and simmer for 3 to 5 minutes or till noodles are tender.

● To serve, ladle stew into individual bowls. If desired, sprinkle with Parmesan cheese. Makes 4 servings.

**Quick Old-Fashioned
Tomato-Beef Stew**
(see recipe, page 39)

Louisiana-Style Chicken 'n' Sausage Gumbo

We found bulk sausage faster to use than sausage links, because we didn't have to slice it.

½ pound bulk Italian sausage
1 cup frozen chopped onion (see tip, page 12)
½ cup frozen chopped green pepper (see tip, page 12)
1½ cups quick-cooking rice
1 14½-ounce can tomatoes
1 cup chicken broth
1 cup frozen cut okra
1 teaspoon bottled minced garlic *or* ¼ teaspoon garlic powder
½ teaspoon dried thyme, crushed
¼ teaspoon bottled hot pepper sauce
2 cups frozen diced cooked chicken *or* two 6-ounce packages frozen cooked shrimp
1 teaspoon filé powder

● Break sausage into large pieces while adding it to a large skillet. Cook sausage, frozen onion, and frozen green pepper over high heat till meat is brown and cooked through, and vegetables are tender. Drain off fat.

● While the meat is cooking, cook the rice according to package directions. Cut up tomatoes.

● Stir *undrained* tomatoes, chicken broth, frozen okra, garlic, thyme, and hot pepper sauce into sausage mixture. Bring to boiling, then reduce heat. Cover and simmer for 5 minutes.

● Stir frozen chicken or shrimp into tomato mixture. Return to boiling. Cover and boil gently for 2 to 3 minutes or just till chicken or shrimp is heated through. Remove skillet from heat, then stir in filé powder.

● To serve, spoon gumbo mixture over hot rice in individual soup bowls. Makes 4 servings.

Oriental Chicken-Noodle Soup

Take your choice—serve this tasty soup as a main dish for three or a side dish for six.

2 14½-ounce cans chicken broth
1 tablespoon soy sauce
1 tablespoon lemon juice
Dash ground ginger
2 cups loose-pack frozen mixed broccoli, carrots, and onions
½ ounce medium egg noodles
1½ cups frozen diced cooked chicken

● In a large saucepan combine broth, soy sauce, lemon juice, and ginger. Bring to boiling, then add frozen vegetables and noodles. Return to boiling, then reduce heat. Cover and simmer for 5 minutes.

● Add frozen chicken. Return to boiling again, then reduce heat. Cover and simmer about 3 minutes more or till vegetables and noodles are tender. Makes 3 servings.

Chicken-Corn Chowder

Transform a can of cheese soup into a hearty corn chowder.

¼ cup frozen chopped onion (see tip, page 12)
¼ cup frozen chopped green pepper (see tip, page 12)
1 tablespoon butter *or* margarine
2 cups frozen diced cooked chicken
1 11-ounce can condensed cheddar cheese soup
1 soup can of milk (1⅓ cups)
1 8¾-ounce can cream-style corn
Cooked bacon pieces (optional)

● In a large saucepan cook the frozen onion and frozen green pepper in butter or margarine over medium-high heat till tender but not brown, stirring occasionally.

● Stir in frozen chicken, cheese soup, milk, and corn. Bring to boiling, stirring constantly.

● To serve, ladle soup into individual bowls. If desired, sprinkle with bacon pieces. Makes 3 servings.

Apple-Curry Chicken Soup

Curry powder, a blend of many spices, gives this creamy soup a mouth-warming spiciness.

¼ cup cornstarch
2 tablespoons curry powder
4 cups chicken broth
2 cups frozen diced cooked chicken
½ of a 16-ounce jar (about ¾ cup) chunk-style applesauce
Peanuts *or* croutons
1 8-ounce carton dairy sour cream

● In a large saucepan stir together cornstarch and curry powder. Then stir in *½ cup* of the chicken broth. Add the remaining broth, frozen chicken, and applesauce.

● Cook and stir the mixture over high heat till thickened and bubbly. Reduce heat to medium. Then cook and stir for 2 minutes more. Meanwhile, if using peanuts for garnish, chop them.

● Gradually stir about 1 cup of the hot mixture into the sour cream, then return the sour cream mixture to the saucepan. Heat through. *Do not boil.*

● To serve, ladle soup into individual soup bowls. Top with chopped peanuts or croutons. Makes 4 servings.

Country Chicken 'n' Biscuits

1　10¾-ounce can condensed
　　cream of chicken soup
¾　cup milk
½　teaspoon dried marjoram,
　　crushed
2　cups frozen diced cooked
　　chicken
1　10-ounce package frozen
　　mixed vegetables *or*
　　frozen peas and carrots
4　ounces sliced process Swiss
　　or American cheese
4　baking powder biscuits

● In a 10-inch skillet combine the chicken soup, milk, and marjoram. Stir in frozen chicken and vegetables. Bring mixture to boiling, then reduce heat. Cover and simmer for 2 minutes. Meanwhile, tear cheese slices into several pieces.

● Stir cheese into chicken mixture and cook till melted. Then place the biscuits on top. Cover. Cook over medium heat for 2 to 3 minutes or till biscuits are heated through. Makes 4 servings.

Country Beef 'n' Biscuits: Prepare the Country Chicken 'n' Biscuits as directed above, *except* substitute one 10¾-ounce can condensed *cream of onion soup,* 12 ounces (about 2 cups) cubed cooked *beef,* and ½ teaspoon dried *thyme,* crushed, for the chicken soup, frozen chicken, and marjoram.

Country Seafood 'n' Biscuits: Prepare Country Chicken 'n' Biscuits as directed above, *except* use ½ *cup* of the milk. Substitute one 10½-ounce can condensed *cream of shrimp soup;* one 12½-ounce can boneless skinless pink *salmon,* drained and broken into chunks; and ¼ teaspoon dried *dillweed* for the chicken soup, frozen chicken, and marjoram.

Warming biscuits
There's no need to warm the biscuits separately. Purchase already-baked biscuits. Then, near the end of cooking, just place them on top of the chicken-vegetable mixture. Cover the skillet and cook for 2 to 3 minutes more or till the biscuits are heated through.

Broccoli and Seafood Chowder

Save a step before dinner by placing the fish in the refrigerator the night before to thaw.

2   cups chicken broth
1   cup frozen cut broccoli
⅛   teaspoon dried thyme,
      crushed
      Dash garlic powder
      Dash pepper
1   8-ounce package frozen
      salad-style crab-flavored
      fish
1   12-ounce can (1½ cups)
      evaporated milk
2   tablespoons all-purpose
      flour
½   cup shredded Swiss cheese
      (2 ounces)

● In a large saucepan combine chicken broth, frozen broccoli, thyme, garlic powder, and pepper. Bring to boiling, then reduce heat. Cover and simmer for 5 minutes.

● While broth mixture is cooking, place frozen crab-flavored fish in a colander. Run *warm water* over fish just till thawed enough to separate, then drain. Cut up any of the large pieces. Combine evaporated milk and flour.

● Stir crab and milk-flour mixture into broth mixture. Cook and stir over medium-high heat till thickened and bubbly. Add cheese. Cook and stir for 1 minute more. Makes 3 or 4 servings.

Tomato-Vegetable Soup with Shrimp

Sherry, tomato, and shrimp—together they result in a rich elegant soup.

2   cups loose-pack frozen
      mixed French cut green
      beans, broccoli,
      mushrooms, and red
      peppers
1   10¾-ounce can condensed
      chicken broth
⅛   teaspoon onion powder
1   24-ounce can (3 cups)
      tomato juice
¼   cup dry sherry
2   6-ounce packages frozen
      cooked shrimp *or* 2 cups
      frozen diced cooked
      chicken
      Green onion, frozen snipped
      chives, *or* croutons
      (optional)

● In a large saucepan combine frozen vegetables, chicken broth, and onion powder. Bring to boiling, then reduce heat. Cover and simmer for 5 minutes.

● Stir in tomato juice. Bring to boiling. Then stir in sherry and frozen shrimp or chicken. Return to boiling. Boil gently about 2 minutes or just till the shrimp or chicken is heated through. Meanwhile, if using green onion for topping, slice it.

● To serve, ladle soup into individual soup bowls. If desired, top with onion, chives, or croutons. Makes 4 servings.

Cauliflower Chowder

The smaller the pieces, the faster they'll cook. So once the cauliflower comes to boiling, use a fork to break up the frozen block.

1   10-ounce package frozen
    cauliflower
½ cup hot water
2   10¾-ounce cans condensed
    cream of potato soup
2   cups milk
1   cup shredded Swiss cheese
    (4 ounces)
⅛ teaspoon ground nutmeg
    Plain croutons (optional)

● In a large saucepan combine the frozen cauliflower and hot water. Bring to boiling, then reduce heat. Cover and simmer about 5 minutes or till tender. *Do not drain.* Using a potato masher, slightly mash the cauliflower.

● Stir in potato soup, milk, cheese, and nutmeg. Cook and stir over high heat about 3½ minutes or till heated through.

● To serve, ladle soup into individual soup bowls. If desired, top with croutons. Makes 4 servings.

Vegetable and Cashew Soup

Cheese, cashews, and northern beans add protein to this meatless, chili-flavored soup. (Pictured on page 10.)

2   cups loose-pack frozen
    mixed zucchini, carrots,
    cauliflower, lima beans,
    and Italian beans
1¼ cups hot water
1   teaspoon instant chicken
    bouillon granules
1   bay leaf
1   15-ounce can great northern
    beans *or* navy beans
1   8-ounce can tomato sauce
¼ cup dry red wine
1   teaspoon sugar
1   teaspoon chili powder
1   cup shredded cheddar *or*
    Monterey Jack cheese
    (4 ounces)
½ cup cashews

● In a large saucepan combine the frozen vegetables, hot water, bouillon granules, and bay leaf. Bring to boiling, then reduce heat. Cover and simmer for 5 minutes. *Do not drain.*

● Stir in *undrained* beans, tomato sauce, wine, sugar, and chili powder. Bring to boiling. Reduce heat. Cover and simmer for 3 minutes. Remove from heat, then remove bay leaf.

● To serve, ladle soup into individual bowls, then top with cheese and cashews. Serves 4 to 6.

FULL-MEAL SALADS

20 MIN

Nutritious and light—now that's a salad! And our main-dish salads fill the bill. We've combined lots of fresh vegetables and fruits to give you quick dinner ideas that are not only easy to make, but are good for you, too.

On-Hand Salad Greens

A tossed salad can round out most any meal. To get one on the table fast, serve greens and vegetables from the take-out salad bar at the supermarket. Or, keep on hand one of our make-ahead mixtures at right.

When storing the torn salad greens, refrigerate them in a sealed plastic bag or a covered plastic container. Place a white paper towel in the bottom of the bag or container to absorb any excess water from the greens.

For maximum freshness of greens, prepare only as much as you can use in two or three days.

Hearty Greens Mix: Combine 2 cups torn *romaine*, 2 cups torn *iceberg lettuce*, and 1 cup torn *curly endive*. Toss to mix. Makes 5 cups.

Spring Greens Mix: Combine 3 cups torn *spinach or sorrel*, 2 cups torn *Bibb or Boston lettuce*, and ½ cup coarsely shredded *carrot*. Toss lightly to mix. Makes about 5 cups.

Timesaving Gadgets

There are lots of kitchen gadgets that can help you short-cut salad making. Here are a few of them:

A *carrot stick maker* to cut sticks in a jiffy.

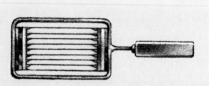

A *tomato slicer* to make beautiful, even slices.

A *wedger* to core and wedge apples or pears.

A *salad spinner* to remove excess water from greens.

An *egg wedger or slicer* to make perfect pieces.

Mexicali Beef 'n' Pasta Salads

Our formula for quick-chilling hot pasta: 2 parts water + 1 part ice cubes.

1 cup elbow, wagon wheel, *or* tiny shell macaroni
12 ounces cooked boneless beef *or* fully cooked turkey breast
1 2¼-ounce can sliced pitted ripe olives
Iceberg lettuce
1 medium tomato (optional)
1 15-ounce can chili beans in chili gravy
½ cup sour cream dip with green chilies
½ cup shredded cheddar cheese (2 ounces)

● Cook the pasta according to package directions, *except* use a 3-quart saucepan and 3½ cups *hot* water. Drain pasta, then transfer it to a large bowl of *ice water.* Let stand for 2 minutes. Then drain well and remove unmelted ice cubes.

● While the pasta is cooking and chilling, cut beef or turkey into ½-inch cubes (you should have about 2 cups). Drain the olives. Shred enough lettuce to line 4 salad plates. If using tomato for garnish, cut it into 8 wedges.

● In a large mixing bowl combine chilled pasta, beef or turkey, olives, and *undrained* beans. Add dip. Toss lightly to coat.

● For salads, line salad plates with the shredded lettuce. Spoon pasta mixture onto the plates, then top with cheese. If desired, garnish with tomato wedges. Makes 4 servings.

From-the-Deli Beef Salads

Just one stop on your way home and you've got the ingredients for a fresh, crispy main dish.

1 cup small whole fresh mushrooms *or* cherry tomatoes
7 cups torn mixed salad greens (see tip, opposite)
12 ounces thinly sliced cooked beef, fully cooked ham, fully cooked turkey breast, *or* a combination
1 pint (2 cups) deli marinated mixed vegetable salad
Croutons (optional)

● Cut mushrooms or cherry tomatoes in half.

● For salads, place greens on salad plates. Roll up each slice of meat. Arrange the meat and mushrooms or tomatoes on top of the greens. Then spoon *undrained* marinated vegetables on top of the greens. If desired, top with croutons. Makes 4 servings.

Turkey Véronique Salads

Turkey Véronique Salads

Belgian endive, also known as witloof chicory, has a mild sweet flavor.

1 cup strawberries *or* one
    10½-ounce can mandarin
    orange sections
1½ cups seedless green grapes
2 heads Belgian endive
    Bibb *or* Boston lettuce
    leaves
12 ounces sliced fully cooked
    smoked turkey breast *or*
    plain turkey breast
    Creamy buttermilk, green
    goddess, *or* blue cheese
    salad dressing
⅓ cup sliced almonds

● Cut strawberries in half or drain mandarin oranges. In a medium mixing bowl combine strawberries or oranges and grapes, then set aside. Separate leaves of Belgian endive.

● For the salads, line salad plates with Belgian endive and Bibb or Boston lettuce leaves. Then arrange turkey and fruit on top. Drizzle salad dressing over the salads. Sprinkle with the sliced almonds. Makes 4 servings.

Chicken Salad on Melon

Keep a can of tuna or salmon on hand in the refrigerator, and you'll always be ready to serve a cool and refreshing last-minute meal.

1 medium cantaloupe *or*
    honeydew melon
1 cup small strawberries
    or seedless red grapes
2 5½-ounce cans chunk-style
    chicken, one 9¼-ounce
    can tuna (water pack), *or*
    one 12½-ounce can bone-
    less skinless pink salmon
1 pint (2 cups) deli creamy
    coleslaw

● To peel melon, cut melon lengthwise in half. Remove seeds. Then cut each melon-half lengthwise in half again. Remove peel from pieces. Cut each melon quarter into 3 slices. Set aside.

● Cut the strawberries or grapes in half. Drain the chicken, tuna, or salmon. In a medium mixing bowl combine chicken, tuna, or salmon and coleslaw. Toss lightly to coat. Add strawberries or grapes, then toss lightly again.

● For salads, overlap the melon slices on salad plates. Spoon the chicken mixture on top. Makes 4 servings.

Shopping at The Deli

When there's no time to cook, depend on the the deli for help. In our recipes, we used sliced deli-cooked beef or turkey breast, and deli-made creamy coleslaw, potato salad, pasta salad, or marinated vegetables.

5-Minute Tuna-Mac

1 3¾-ounce can tuna (water pack)
4 large radishes
1 pint (2 cups) deli creamy macaroni salad

● Drain tuna and slice radishes. In a medium mixing bowl combine the tuna, radishes, and macaroni salad. If necessary, stir in 1 tablespoon *mayonnaise or salad dressing* to moisten. Makes 2 servings.

Seafood-Tomato Tulips

8 ounces crab-flavored fish sticks
1 cup shredded cabbage
½ cup creamy cucumber salad dressing
  Several dashes bottled hot pepper sauce
2 medium tomatoes
  Lettuce leaves

● For fish mixture, chop crab-flavored fish sticks. In a medium mixing bowl combine fish, cabbage, salad dressing, and hot pepper sauce. Toss lightly till well mixed.

● For tomato cups, cut out ½ inch of the core from each tomato. Invert tomatoes. Cutting from top to, *but not through,* the stem end, cut each tomato into 6 wedges.

● For salads, line salad plates with lettuce leaves. Place the tomatoes on the plates. Spread wedges slightly apart, then fill with the fish mixture. Makes 2 servings.

Making tomato cups
Choose bright red, medium tomatoes. Insert the point of a sharp knife into each tomato near the core and cut out ½ inch of the core. Invert the tomatoes. Then cut from the top to, *but not through,* the stem end. Repeat to cut each tomato into 6 wedges, as shown at right.

To fill the tomato cups, spread the wedges apart, then spoon in the fish mixture.

Dilly Deli Salmon-Potato Salad

Save time by choosing the canned salmon that already has the skin and bones removed.

2 hard-cooked eggs (see tip, page 56) *or* 1 medium tomato (optional)

1 2¼-ounce can sliced pitted ripe olives *or* ½ cup pimiento-stuffed green olives

1 12½-ounce can boneless skinless pink salmon

1½ pints (3 cups) deli creamy potato salad

½ teaspoon dried dillweed
   Lettuce leaves

● If using eggs or tomato for garnish, remove shells from eggs and cut eggs or tomato into wedges. Set wedges aside.

● Drain olives and salmon. In a medium mixing bowl combine olives, potato salad, and dillweed. Toss lightly till mixed. Break salmon into large chunks while adding it to the potato salad mixture in bowl. Toss lightly to coat.

● For salads, line salad plates with lettuce leaves. Spoon potato mixture onto the plates. If desired, garnish with egg or tomato wedges. Makes 4 servings.

Italian Tortellini Salad

Team pasta with crispy greens as the base for a great one-dish meal. (Pictured on page 8.)

2 cups loose-pack frozen mixed broccoli, carrots, and cauliflower, *or* one 9-ounce package frozen artichoke hearts

4 ounces provolone cheese *or* mozzarella cheese

1 2¼-ounce can sliced pitted ripe olives

4 cups torn mixed salad greens (see tip, page 48)

1 pint (2 cups) deli marinated tortellini salad

1 3½-ounce package sliced pepperoni

¼ cup grated *or* finely shredded Parmesan cheese
   Clear Italian dressing (optional)

● Place frozen vegetables in a colander. Run *hot water* over vegetables just till thawed. Drain well.

● While vegetables are draining, cut provolone or mozzarella cheese into ½-inch cubes. Drain olives.

● For salad, in a large salad bowl combine drained vegetables, cheese cubes, olives, salad greens, *undrained* tortellini salad, pepperoni slices, and Parmesan cheese. Toss lightly to coat. If necessary, add enough of the Italian dressing to coat. If desired, sprinkle with additional Parmesan cheese. Makes 4 servings.

Toss-Your-Own Salad

Create any salad that suits your fancy.

1 cup Vegetable *or* Fruit
    Option, *or* a combination
1 Meat, Poultry, Fish, *or* Egg
    Option
4 ounces sliced Cheese Option
4 cups torn mixed salad
    greens (see tip, page 48)
Desired salad dressing
1 Topping Option

● For Vegetable or Fruit Option: If using carrots, celery, cucumber or zucchini, or mushrooms, slice them. If using tomato, cut it into 8 wedges, then cut the wedges crosswise in half. If using frozen vegetables, place them in a colander. Run *hot water* over them just till thawed, then drain well. If using the canned mandarin oranges, pineapple, or fruits for salad, drain it well.

● For Meat, Poultry, Fish, or Egg Option: If using beef, turkey, or ham, cut it into cubes (you should have about 1⅓ cups). If using crab sticks, cut them into 1½-inch pieces. If using salmon or tuna, drain and break it into large chunks. If using eggs, remove shells and cut them into wedges.

● For Cheese Option, cut slices into bite-size strips.

● For salad, in a large salad bowl combine desired vegetable or fruit, meat, and cheese options, and salad greens. Pour salad dressing over greens mixture. Toss lightly to coat. Sprinkle with desired Topping Option. Makes 3 or 4 servings.

Vegetable or Fruit Options	Meat, Poultry, Fish, or Egg Options	Cheese Options
2 medium carrots	8 ounces cooked boneless beef	American cheese
2 stalks celery	8 ounces fully cooked turkey breast	cheddar cheese
½ of a medium cucumber *or* zucchini	8 ounces fully cooked boneless ham	Swiss cheese
8 large mushrooms	8 ounces crab-flavored fish sticks	
1 large tomato	1 6½-ounce can boneless skinless pink salmon *or* tuna (water pack)	**Topping Options**
1 cup fresh broccoli *or* cauliflower flowerets	4 hard-cooked eggs (see tip, page 56)	sunflower nuts
1 cup loose-pack frozen mixed broccoli, carrots, and cauliflower		croutons
1 16-ounce can mandarin orange sections		cooked bacon pieces
1 15¼-ounce can pineapple chunks (juice pack)		crushed canned French-fried onions
1 17-ounce can fruits for salad		grated *or* finely shredded Parmesan cheese

HEARTY SANDWICHES

20 MIN

Some like their sandwiches hot and some like them cold. We've got both. No matter which of our ten sandwiches you choose, you'll have it on the table in a flash.

Sandwich Tips

Warming Tortillas

Do your tortillas crack as you roll them up? Here's how to prevent the problem.

Often just letting the tortillas stand at room temperature will help. Or, you can warm them in either the conventional or microwave oven.

● *Conventional oven method:* Wrap about 8 tortillas in a piece of foil. Place the wrapped tortillas in a 350° oven about 5 minutes or until they're heated through.

● *Microwave oven method:* Place about 4 tortillas between damp white paper towels. Micro-cook the tortillas on 100% power (high) about 30 seconds to 1 minute or until they're heated through.

Hard-Cooked Eggs Anytime

For those times when you need a quick snack, a garnish, or something extra in a sandwich or salad, keep a supply of hard-cooked eggs on hand. Cook several eggs at once, then refrigerate them, covered, for up to 1 week.

To hard-cook eggs, place them in a saucepan. Add enough water to cover. Bring to boiling, then reduce the heat to just below simmering. Cover and cook the eggs for 15 to 20 minutes.

To cool the eggs quickly, pour off the hot water and fill the saucepan with *ice water*. Let stand at least 2 minutes.

The shells will be easier to remove if you shell the eggs before storing them in the refrigerator. This also means you won't have to do it at the last minute.

When you're in a real pinch, you can often buy hard-cooked eggs at the deli. Usually they're still in their shells, so plan on a few extra minutes to shell them.

Grilled Beef 'n' Cheese Sandwiches

1 16-ounce jar sweet-sour
    cabbage *or* one 16-ounce
    can sauerkraut
    Horseradish mustard
8 slices dark rye bread
8 ounces sliced cooked beef
4 slices Swiss cheese
1 tablespoon butter *or*
    margarine

● Drain the sweet-sour cabbage. Or, rinse and drain the sauerkraut. Then set cabbage or sauerkraut aside.

● Preheat griddle over medium-high heat. Meanwhile, spread mustard on one side of bread slices. Top mustard side of *half* of the bread slices with beef and cabbage or sauerkraut, then cheese. Top sandwiches with remaining bread slices.

● Melt butter or margarine on griddle. (If necessary, add more butter to grill second side.) Place sandwiches on hot griddle. Grill for 2 to 3 minutes or till toasted, turning once. Serves 4.

Skillet Fajitas

8   6-inch flour tortillas
1   small tomato (optional)
    Iceberg lettuce (optional)
12 ounces beef flank steak
1   tablespoon cooking oil
½   cup salsa
½   cup dairy sour cream
½   cup shredded cheddar
    cheese (2 ounces)

● If desired, warm tortillas according to tip directions opposite. Meanwhile, if using the tomato and lettuce for toppings, chop the tomato and shred enough lettuce to make about 1 cup.

● Preheat a large skillet over high heat. Meanwhile, thinly slice steak on the bias into bite-size strips. Add cooking oil to the hot skillet. (If necessary, add more oil during cooking.) Then add beef to the skillet. Cook and stir beef over high heat for 2 to 3 minutes or till done. Stir in salsa. Cook and stir till heated through. Transfer meat mixture to a serving bowl.

● To serve, let everyone assemble their own fajitas. For each fajita, spoon some of the meat mixture across the center of a tortilla (within 1 inch of one side). Then top with sour cream and cheese. If desired, also top with tomato and lettuce. Roll the tortilla around meat and toppings. Makes 4 servings.

Corned Beef Pockets

½ cup frozen peas
1 2½-ounce package very
    thinly sliced corned beef
1 cup shredded cabbage
½ cup shredded mozzarella
    cheese (2 ounces)
¼ teaspoon caraway seed
¼ cup Thousand Island salad
    dressing
2 large pita bread rounds

● Place frozen peas in a colander. Run *hot water* over peas just till thawed, then drain well. Chop corned beef. In a medium mixing bowl combine peas, corned beef, cabbage, and cheese. Stir caraway seed into Thousand Island dressing, then pour over cabbage mixture. Toss lightly to coat.

● To serve, cut pita bread rounds crosswise in half, then open pita pockets. Spoon cabbage mixture into pockets. Serves 2.

Smorrebrod

Smorrebrod

Pronounced SMAWRUH-brahd, these main-dish, piled-high, open-face sandwiches are a national Danish passion.

1 Meat, Poultry, *or* Fish Option
1 Vegetable Option
   Soft *or* whipped margarine, *or* soft-style cream cheese (optional)
4 thin slices Bread Option
   Lettuce leaves *or* alfalfa sprouts
4 ounces sliced Cheese Option
1 Condiment Option (optional)
   Fresh herb spigs (optional)
   Capers (optional)

● For Meat, Poultry, or Fish Option: If using frozen shrimp, place it in a colander. Run *cool water* over shrimp just till thawed. Drain shrimp well. If using salmon, drain and flake it.

● For Vegetable Option, slice enough for 4 sandwiches.

● To assemble sandwiches, if desired, spread margarine or cream cheese on one side of bread slices. Top with lettuce leaves or sprouts. Then top with meat, poultry, or fish, and cheese. If desired, dollop with condiment. Then top with vegetable. If desired, garnish with herbs or capers. Makes 4 servings.

Meat, Poultry, *or* Fish Options

12 ounces sliced cooked beef
12 ounces sliced fully cooked turkey breast
12 ounces sliced fully cooked ham
12 ounces thinly sliced corned beef *or* pastrami
1 12-ounce package braunschweiger slices
1 8-ounce package frozen cooked shrimp
1 12½-ounce can boneless skinless pink salmon

Vegetable Options

radishes
small cucumber
cherry tomatoes
sweet pickle slices
small onion

Bread Options

white bread
French bread
light *or* dark rye bread
pumpernickel bread
whole wheat bread

Cheese Options

Havarti cheese
Swiss cheese
mozzarella cheese
provolone cheese
Monterey Jack cheese
brick cheese
cheddar cheese

Condiment Options

mayonnaise *or* salad dressing
mustard-mayonnaise sandwich and salad sauce
cream-style prepared horseradish
horseradish mustard
Dijon-style mustard

Turkey Tortillas

1 small carrot
1 tablespoon milk
1 teaspoon curry powder
½ of an 8-ounce container soft-style cream cheese with chives and onion
4 6-inch flour tortillas
8 lettuce leaves
3 2½-ounce packages very thinly sliced smoked turkey

● Coarsely shred carrot, then set aside. In a small mixing bowl combine milk and curry powder. Then stir in cream cheese till well blended.

● To assemble, spread one-fourth of the cream cheese mixture onto one side of each tortilla. Top with shredded carrot, then top with lettuce leaves and turkey. Fold tortillas in half and secure with wooden toothpicks. Makes 4 servings.

Bratwurst Pattie Melts

Panfrying the patties works just as well as broiling—just follow the package directions. Add cheese before you finish cooking, cover the skillet, and cook until the cheese melts.

4 uncooked bratwurst patties (about 12 ounces total)
1 8-ounce can sauerkraut (optional)
2 tablespoons dairy sour cream
1 tablespoon brown mustard *or* Dijon-style mustard
½ teaspoon caraway seed
8 slices pumpernickel bread *or* 4 whole wheat hamburger buns
4 slices process Swiss cheese

● Preheat broiler. Meanwhile, place bratwurst patties on the unheated rack of the broiler pan. If using the sauerkraut for topping, rinse and drain it, then set aside.

● Broil patties according to the package directions, *except* turn patties over once. Meanwhile, in a bowl stir together sour cream, mustard, and caraway seed. Spread mixture on one side of bread slices. Or, split buns and spread mixture on insides.

● Place a slice of cheese on each cooked pattie. Broil about 30 seconds more or till cheese is melted. Serve patties on bread or bottom halves of buns. If desired, top with sauerkraut. Then add remaining bread slices or bun tops. Makes 4 servings.

Tarragon Chicken-Salad Pitas

1½ cups frozen diced cooked chicken
½ cup seedless grapes
¼ cup mayonnaise *or* salad dressing
2 to 3 teaspoons milk
¼ teaspoon dried tarragon, crushed
2 large pita bread rounds
Lettuce leaves

● Place chicken in a clear plastic bag. Seal tightly. Place bag in a bowl of *hot water* about 5 minutes or till partially thawed.

● While chicken is thawing, cut grapes in half. Stir together mayonnaise or salad dressing, milk, and tarragon. Add chicken and grapes. Toss to coat. Season to taste with *salt* and *pepper.*

● To serve, cut pitas crosswise in half, then open and line *3 halves* with lettuce leaves. (Reserve the remaining pita half for another use.) Spoon chicken mixture into pockets. Serves 3.

Chicken-Salad Sandwich Loaf

Parties are for loafing around. So here's a festive sandwich that feeds a crowd and lets you take it easy.

2 6¾-ounce cans chunk-style
   chicken *or* one 12½-ounce
   can boneless skinless
   pink salmon
1 small tomato
⅓ cup mayonnaise *or* salad
   dressing
¼ cup bacon and tomato *or*
   sour cream and bacon
   salad dressing
1 6-ounce package shredded
   Swiss cheese (1½ cups)
1 1-pound loaf unsliced
   pumpernickel *or* rye
   bread
   Leaf lettuce

● Drain and flake chicken or salmon, then chop tomato. In a medium mixing bowl stir together the mayonnaise and bacon salad dressing. Add chicken or salmon, tomato, and cheese. Toss lightly to mix.

● To assemble sandwich loaf, cut bread into ½-inch-thick slices by cutting from the top to, *but not through,* the bottom forming pockets. Line the first pocket with lettuce, then line *every other* pocket. Spoon chicken mixture into every lettuce-lined pocket.

● To serve, cut into sandwiches by cutting apart the unfilled pockets. Makes 6 to 8 servings.

Assembling the sandwich loaf

Slice the bread into pockets. Spread each slice apart slightly. Line the first pocket with lettuce, then line *every other* pocket with more lettuce. Spoon the chicken mixture into every lettuce-lined pocket.

   To serve the sandwich loaf, cut the loaf into individual sandwiches by cutting the unfilled pockets apart.

61

Barbecued Chicken-Strip Sandwiches

Sweet-sour barbecued chicken for two—without leftovers.

8 ounces boned skinless
   chicken breast halves,
   turkey breast tenderloins,
   or lean boneless pork
⅓ cup chili sauce
2 tablespoons currant *or*
   grape jelly, *or* red plum
   jam
1 tablespoon vinegar
1 tablespoon prepared
   mustard
   Several dashes bottled hot
   pepper sauce (optional)
1 tablespoon cooking oil
2 kaiser rolls *or* two 6-inch-
   long French-style rolls
1 medium carrot (optional)
   Potato chips (optional)

● Thinly slice poultry or pork into bite-size strips, then set aside. Preheat a medium skillet over medium-high heat.

● While skillet is heating, for sauce mixture, in a small mixing bowl stir together chili sauce, jelly or jam, vinegar, mustard, and hot pepper sauce, if desired. Set sauce mixture aside.

● Add oil to the hot skillet. Then add meat. Cook and stir over medium-high heat for 2 to 3 minutes or till poultry is just tender or pork is no longer pink. Stir in sauce mixture. Bring to boiling. Reduce heat. Cover and simmer for 5 minutes. Meanwhile, split rolls. If serving carrot, cut it into sticks.

● To serve, spoon meat mixture on bottom halves of rolls. Add roll tops. If desired, serve with carrot sticks and potato chips. Makes 2 servings.

To micro-cook: Slice poultry or pork and combine sauce mixture as directed above. Omit oil. Place poultry or pork in a 1-quart microwave-safe casserole. Cover. Micro-cook on 100% power (high) for 2 to 4 minutes or till meat is no longer pink, stirring once. Drain off liquid, then stir in the sauce mixture. Cook, covered, on high about 2 minutes more or till meat is tender and sauce is heated through, stirring once. Meanwhile, split rolls. If serving carrot, cut it into sticks. Serve as above.

Curried Egg- 'n' Cheese-Salad Pitas

Chop the eggs with a pastry blender—it's a fast way to break them up.

1 small tomato
4 hard-cooked eggs (see tip,
   page 56)
½ cup cream-style cottage
   cheese
½ of a 2¼-ounce can sliced
   pitted ripe olives
½ of a stalk celery
2 tablespoons mayonnaise *or*
   salad dressing
1 to 2 teaspoons curry powder
¼ teaspoon onion salt
⅛ to ¼ teaspoon pepper
2 large pita bread rounds *or*
   4 croissants

● Slice tomato, then set aside. If necessary, remove shells from eggs. Drain cottage cheese and olives. Chop celery.

● Place eggs in a medium mixing bowl. Using a pastry blender or potato masher, chop eggs. Add the drained cottage cheese, mayonnaise or salad dressing, curry powder, onion salt, and pepper. Stir till well blended. Then stir in olives and celery.

● To serve, cut pita bread rounds crosswise in half, then open pita pockets. Or, split croissants. Line insides of pita pockets or bottom halves of croissants with tomato slices. Spoon the egg mixture into the pita pockets or onto croissant bottoms. Add croissant tops. Makes 4 servings.

MAKE-AHEAD FREEZER MIX

20 MIN

With our culinary math, one basic freezer meat mix equals six different delicious dinners. Just spend a little time cooking ahead and you'll be surprised how quickly and easily you can serve a home-cooked meal.

Make-Ahead Meat Mixture

Plan ahead—keep plain, curry-, chili-, and Italian-seasoned meat mixtures on hand for quick, hassle-free meals.

1 egg
½ cup fresh *or* frozen chopped onion (see tip, page 12)
3 to 5 teaspoons curry powder *or* chili powder, *or* 1 to 1½ teaspoons Italian seasoning, crushed (optional)
½ teaspoon salt
¼ teaspoon pepper
2 pounds *fresh* ground raw turkey *or* lean ground beef
½ cup soft bread crumbs

● In a large bowl use a fork to slightly beat egg. Add onion. If desired, stir in curry powder, chili powder, or Italian seasoning. Then stir in salt and pepper. Add meat and bread crumbs. (If using ground beef, omit the bread crumbs.) Mix well.

● To freeze, on 4 pieces of freezer plastic wrap form the meat into four ½-inch-thick rectangles. Then wrap, seal, label, and freeze. Before using the meat in the recipes in this chapter, thaw packages of meat in the refrigerator or in the microwave oven. Makes 4 (8-ounce) packages.

● *To thaw in refrigerator:* The night before, place the wrapped frozen meat block in a baking dish in the refrigerator.

● *To thaw in microwave oven:* Place one frozen unwrapped meat block in a baking dish. Cover with vented microwave-safe plastic wrap. Micro-cook on 30% power (medium-low) for 2½ minutes. Rotate dish a quarter-turn. Cook, covered, on medium-low about 2½ minutes more or till thawed but not cooked.

Packaging the meat mixture
Use only *fresh* ground meat for the meat mixture. Do not use meat that has been frozen before.

Divide the meat mixture into 4 portions. Then form each portion into a ½-inch-thick rectangle on *freezer* plastic wrap. This clear plastic material is sturdier than everyday plastic wrap. Read the label to make sure your wrap is freezer-safe. Or, use laminated wrap (also known as freezer paper).

Wrap each rectangle securely using a double fold. Then seal, label, and freeze the packages of meat. As a general guide, you can freeze the meat mixture for up to 3 months.

Pizza Pie

1 8-ounce package plain,
    chili-, *or* Italian-seasoned
    frozen Make-Ahead Meat
    Mixture
1 4-ounce package (4)
    refrigerated crescent rolls
1 tablespoon cooking oil
¼ cup frozen chopped green
    pepper (see tip, page 12)
1 2½-ounce jar sliced
    mushrooms
1 2¼-ounce can sliced pitted
    ripe olives
1 8-ounce can pizza sauce
½ cup shredded mozzarella
    cheese, cheddar cheese, *or*
    a combination (2 ounces
    total)

● Thaw meat according to directions opposite. Before preparing pizza, preheat oven to 375°.

● To prepare pizza, separate crescent rolls into 4 triangles. Place triangles in an ungreased 7-inch pie plate or 8-inch cast-iron skillet. Press the dough over the bottom and up the sides of the pie plate or skillet, forming a crust. Bake crust in the 375° oven about 8 minutes or till lightly brown. (Crust will be puffy.)

● While crust is baking, if using turkey, preheat a large skillet over high heat and add cooking oil. (If using beef, omit preheating and the oil.) Break the thawed meat into large pieces while adding it to the skillet. Cook meat and frozen green pepper over high heat till turkey is no longer pink or beef is brown and green pepper is tender. Then drain off fat. Meanwhile, drain the mushrooms and olives. Then stir mushrooms, olives, and pizza sauce into cooked meat mixture. Cook till heated through.

● Spoon *hot* sauce mixture on top of *hot* crust. Then sprinkle with cheese. Return pizza to oven. Bake about 5 minutes more or till cheese is melted. Makes 2 or 3 servings.

International Stroganoff

Make it an American, Indian, Mexican, or Italian dinner tonight by just changing the meat mixture to change the flavor.

2 8-ounce packages frozen
    Make-Ahead Meat Mixture
    (plain *or* with any
    seasoning)
6 ounces wide noodles
1 tablespoon cooking oil
1 4-ounce can mushroom
    stems and pieces
1 7¾-ounce can semi-
    condensed cream of
    mushroom soup
¼ cup hot water
1 8-ounce container dairy
    sour cream
1 tablespoon all-purpose flour
2 tablespoons dry white wine
    Fresh parsley (optional)

● Thaw meat according to directions opposite.

● Cook the pasta according to package directions, *except* use a 3-quart saucepan and 6 cups *hot* water. Then drain.

● While pasta is cooking, if using turkey, preheat a large skillet over high heat. Add cooking oil. (If using beef, omit preheating and the oil.) Break the thawed meat into large pieces while adding it to the skillet. Cook meat over high heat till turkey is no longer pink or beef is brown. Then drain off fat.

● While meat is cooking, drain the mushrooms. Then stir the mushrooms, soup, and hot water into the cooked meat. Bring mixture to boiling. Meanwhile, combine sour cream and flour.

● Stir sour cream mixture into meat mixture. Then stir in wine. Cook and stir over medium heat till thickened and bubbly. Cook and stir for 1 minute more. Serve meat mixture over hot pasta. If desired, snip parsley on top. Makes 4 servings.

Taco Salads

Hearty Pasta Soup

Perfect for a cold winter day, this full-meal soup will both warm you and fill you up.

2 8-ounce packages frozen
  Make-Ahead Meat Mixture
  (plain or with any
  seasoning)
1 stalk celery
1 tablespoon cooking oil
½ cup frozen chopped onion
  (see tip, page 12)
1 16-ounce can tomatoes
1 4½-ounce package tiny shell
  macaroni with herb-and-
  tomato sauce
1 tablespoon instant chicken
  or beef bouillon granules

● Thaw meat according to directions on page 64.

● Chop celery, then set aside. If using turkey, preheat a 4-quart Dutch oven over high heat and add cooking oil. (If using beef, omit preheating and the oil.) Break the thawed meat into large pieces while adding it to the Dutch oven. Cook meat, celery, and frozen onion over high heat till turkey is no longer pink or beef is brown and vegetables are tender. Drain off fat.

● While meat is cooking, cut up tomatoes. Stir the *undrained* tomatoes, pasta mix, bouillon granules, and 3½ cups *hot water* into cooked meat mixture. Bring to boiling, then reduce heat. Gently boil, uncovered, about 8 minutes or till the pasta is tender, stirring occasionally. Makes 4 servings.

Taco Salads

Opt for either a hot or mild salad. Just use the kind of taco sauce that you like, but remember the chili powder adds some hotness, too.

Frozen avocado dip
  (optional)
1 8-ounce package plain,
  chili-, *or* Italian-seasoned
  frozen Make-Ahead Meat
  Mixture
1 tablespoon cooking oil
1 8-ounce can red kidney
  beans
1 8-ounce bottle taco sauce
2 small tomatoes
4 cups torn mixed salad
  greens (see tip, page 48)
½ cup shredded cheddar
  cheese (2 ounces)
  Plain tortilla chips *or* corn
  chips
  Dairy sour cream (optional)
  Salsa (optional)

● The night before, if serving avocado dip, place it in the refrigerator to thaw. Thaw meat according to directions on page 64.

● For meat mixture, if using turkey, preheat a large skillet over high heat and add cooking oil. (If using beef, omit preheating and the oil.) Break the thawed meat into large pieces while adding it to the skillet. Cook meat over high heat till turkey is no longer pink or beef is brown, then drain off fat.

● While meat is cooking, drain beans. Then stir beans and taco sauce into the cooked meat. Bring to boiling, then reduce heat. Cover and simmer for 3 minutes.

● While mixture is simmering, cut each tomato into 8 wedges. Place salad greens on large salad plates. Spoon warm meat mixture on top of greens. Sprinkle with cheese. Arrange tomatoes and chips around outer edges of the plates. If desired, serve with avocado dip, sour cream, and salsa. Makes 2 servings.

To micro-cook: Prepare Taco Salads as above, *except* cook meat in microwave oven. Place meat in a 1-quart microwave-safe casserole. Cover. Micro-cook on 100% power (high) for 3 to 5 minutes or till no longer pink, stirring once. Drain. Stir in drained beans and taco sauce. Cook, covered, on high about 3 minutes more or till heated, stirring once. Serve as above.

Mexican Skillet Dinner

1   6-ounce container frozen avocado dip *or* one 8-ounce container sour cream dip with chives
2   8-ounce packages frozen plain *or* chili-seasoned Make-Ahead Meat Mixture
1   tablespoon cooking oil
1   16-ounce can refried beans
1   12-ounce jar salsa
⅛ of a small head iceberg lettuce
1   2¼-ounce can sliced pitted ripe olives
1   cup shredded cheddar *or* Monterey Jack cheese (4 ounces)
2   cups (3 ounces) tortilla chips
    Salsa (optional)

● The night before, if using avocado dip, place it in the refrigerator to thaw. Thaw meat according to directions on page 64.

● For taco mixture, if using turkey, preheat a large skillet over high heat and add cooking oil. (If using beef, omit preheating and the oil.) Break the thawed meat into large pieces while adding it to the skillet. Cook meat over high heat till turkey is no longer pink or beef is brown. Drain off fat. Stir in refried beans and 12-ounce jar of salsa. Bring mixture to boiling. Reduce heat. Cover and simmer for 1 minute. Meanwhile, shred lettuce and drain olives.

● To serve, remove taco mixture from heat and sprinkle with cheese. Slightly crush tortilla chips on top. Then top with shredded lettuce and olives. Dollop with avocado or sour cream dip. If desired, drizzle with additional salsa. Makes 6 servings.

To micro-cook: Thaw dip and meat as above. Omit oil. Place loose ground meat in a 12x7½x2-inch baking dish. Cover with vented microwave-safe plastic wrap. Micro-cook, on 100% power (high) for 4 to 6 minutes or till no pink remains, stirring once. Drain off fat. Then stir in beans and salsa. Cook, uncovered, on high for 7 to 9 minutes or till heated, stirring once or twice. Meanwhile, shred lettuce and drain olives. Serve as above.

Quarter-Pound Burgers

A fast-food feast right out of your own kitchen.

1   8-ounce package frozen Make-Ahead Meat Mixture (plain *or* with any seasoning)
    Tomato, cucumber, onion, *or* a combination
2   hamburger buns *or* kaiser rolls
    Desired condiment (catsup, prepared mustard, salsa, bottled barbecue sauce, mayonnaise *or* salad dressing, plain yogurt *or* dairy sour cream, *or* a combination)
2   lettuce leaves *or* alfalfa sprouts

● Thaw meat according to directions on page 64.

● Unwrap the thawed meat, keeping the rectangle shape. Cut the meat rectangle crosswise in half, forming 2 square patties. Preheat a large skillet over high heat. (If using turkey, lightly grease skillet before heating.) Add meat patties, then reduce heat to medium. Cover and cook for 4 minutes. Turn the patties over. Continue cooking, covered, about 4 minutes or till turkey is well done or till beef is to desired doneness.

● While patties are cooking, slice enough tomato, cucumber, or onion to top 2 burgers. Separate onion slices into rings. Split buns or rolls, then spread bottoms with desired condiment. Serve patties on bun bottoms. If desired, top with additional condiment. Then top with the lettuce or sprouts, and tomato, cucumber, or onion rings. Add bun tops. Makes 2 servings.

MEALTIME EXTRAS

20 MIN

Even though you're in a hurry, don't cheat yourself out of mouth-watering side dishes, breads, or desserts. Most of these quick-to-fix accompaniments take only about 10 minutes to prepare...and can make you feel like you didn't miss a thing.

Spread on the Flavor

With several sweet and savory spreads in your refrigerator, you'll have an ace up your culinary sleeve.

These spreads are quick and they add an extra flavor zing. Keep them on hand to spread on muffins or breads; toss with pasta; or dollop on cooked steaks, fish, or poultry.

To ½ cup *soft or whipped margarine* stir in *one* of the flavorings at right.

FOR A SWEET SPREAD ADD ONE:

2 tablespoons honey

2 tablespoons honey *plus* ¼ cup finely chopped pitted dates

¼ cup sifted powdered sugar *plus* 2 tablespoons frozen orange juice concentrate

FOR A SAVORY SPREAD ADD ONE:

2 tablespoons chopped drained capers *or* anchovy fillets

¼ cup crumbled blue cheese

1 tablespoon snipped fresh basil *or* 1 teaspoon dried basil, crushed

½ teaspoon bottled minced garlic *or* ¼ teaspoon garlic powder

½ teaspoon curry powder

Perk Up Coffee

A good cup of coffee is a wonderful ending to a perfect meal. While you're eating dinner, brew coffee in a percolator or a coffee maker according to the manufacturer's directions, *except* use *2 tablespoons* ground coffee for each ¾ *cup* (6 ounces) water.

After dinner, create your favorite coffee combination by adding *one* of the flavorings at right to each cup. If you like, top each serving with whipped *dairy dessert topping* and sprinkle with ground *cinnamon or nutmeg.*

1 tablespoon chocolate-flavored syrup

1 tablespoon Irish whiskey *plus* 2 teaspoons sugar

1 tablespoon Amaretto

1 tablespoon orange liqueur

70

Bulgur Pilaf

Flecks of carrot and peas add both color and flavor.

1 small carrot
¼ cup frozen peas
¼ cup bulgur
1 teaspoon instant chicken bouillon granules
1 teaspoon butter *or* margarine
⅛ teaspoon onion powder
⅛ teaspoon garlic powder

● Coarsely shred carrot. In a small saucepan combine the shredded carrot, frozen peas, bulgur, chicken bouillon granules, butter or margarine, onion powder, garlic powder, and ½ cup *hot water*.

● Bring to boiling, then reduce heat. Cover and cook mixture over medium heat about 5 minutes or till liquid is absorbed. Makes 2 servings.

Golden Rice with Cashews

Great with broiled pork chops, fish, or chicken.

1½ cups hot water
1 teaspoon instant chicken bouillon granules
⅛ teaspoon onion powder
⅛ teaspoon ground turmeric
1½ cups quick-cooking rice
¾ cup cashews *or* peanuts
1 tablespoon frozen snipped chives

● In a saucepan combine hot water, bouillon, onion powder, and turmeric. Bring to boiling. Remove from heat. Add rice. Cover. Let stand 5 minutes. Stir in nuts and chives. Serves 4.

To micro-cook: Place rice, water, bouillon granules, onion powder, and turmeric in a 1-quart microwave-safe casserole, then cover. Micro-cook at 100% power (high) for 3 to 4 minutes or till bubbly, stirring once. Then let rice stand, covered, for 5 minutes. Stir in nuts and chives.

Pasta-Veggie Toss

Be sure to drain the pasta and vegetables well. Extra water dilutes the dressing.

½ cup tiny shell macaroni *or* other small pasta
1 cup loose-pack frozen mixed zucchini, carrots, cauliflower, lima beans, and Italian beans
1 2¼-ounce can sliced pitted ripe olives
¼ cup creamy Italian *or* creamy cucumber salad dressing

● In a medium covered saucepan bring 2 cups *hot water* to boiling. Add pasta and return to boiling. Reduce heat and gently boil for 4 minutes. Then add frozen vegetables. Return to boiling, then reduce heat. Gently boil about 4 minutes more or till pasta is tender and vegetables are nearly tender. Drain mixture, then transfer it to a large bowl of *ice water*. Let mixture stand for 4 minutes. Drain well and remove any unmelted ice cubes. Meanwhile, drain olives.

● Transfer pasta mixture to a medium bowl. Add olives. Pour dressing over vegetable mixture. Toss lightly to coat. Serves 4.

Herbed Potato Wedges

A quick version of French fries.

2 tablespoons butter *or* margarine
3 medium potatoes (about 1 pound)
¼ teaspoon dried basil, oregano, *or* tarragon, crushed
¼ teaspoon onion salt *or* garlic salt
⅛ teaspoon pepper

● Preheat broiler. Meanwhile, place butter or margarine in a 13x9x2-inch baking pan. Then place pan under preheating broiler until butter or margarine is melted.

● While the broiler is preheating and butter or margarine is melting, scrub potatoes. Then cut each potato into 8 wedges. Stir basil, oregano, or tarragon; onion or garlic salt; and pepper into melted butter or margarine. Then add potato wedges. Stir to coat potatoes with butter mixture.

● Place pan containing potatoes 3 inches from the heat. Broil potatoes for 5 minutes. Using a wide spatula, turn potato wedges over and broil about 5 minutes more or till tender. Makes 4 servings.

To micro-cook: Scrub and cut potatoes as directed above, then set aside. Place butter or margarine in an 8x8x2-inch baking dish. Micro-cook, uncovered, on 100% power (high) about 45 to 60 seconds or till melted. Stir in basil, oregano, or tarragon; onion or garlic salt; and pepper. Then add potato wedges and coat with butter mixture. Cover with vented microwave-safe plastic wrap. Cook on high for 8 to 10 minutes or till tender, stirring twice.

Peppy Cheese-Sauced Corn

Jazz up your favorite vegetable with this zesty cheese sauce.

1 10-ounce package frozen whole kernel corn, brussels sprouts, *or* cauliflower
½ of an 8-ounce container of cheddar-flavored cold-pack cheese food
2 tablespoons canned diced green chili peppers
Dash bottled hot pepper sauce
⅓ cup plain croutons

● Cook frozen vegetables according to package directions, then drain and return vegetables to saucepan.

● Add cheese, chilies, and pepper sauce to hot vegetables. Cook and stir over low heat till cheese is melted and heated through.

● To serve, transfer mixture to a serving bowl. Top with the croutons. Makes 4 servings.

To micro-cook: Place frozen vegetables in a 1½-quart microwave-safe casserole. Sprinkle with 2 tablespoons *water,* then cover. Micro-cook on 100% power (high) for 6 to 9 minutes or till nearly tender, stirring once. Then drain. Spoon on cheese, then add chilies and hot pepper sauce. Cook, covered, on high for ½ to 1 minute more or till cheese is melted, stirring once. Top with croutons.

Creamy Noodles 'n' Vegetables

Bite it—that's the way to check the doneness of pasta. It should be tender yet slightly firm.

5 ounces mafalda (medium-
   size, curly-edge) noodles
   or linguine
1 10-ounce package frozen
   mixed vegetables *or*
   cut broccoli
½ of an 8-ounce container of
   soft-style cream cheese
   with chives and onion
¼ cup milk
   Salt
   Pepper

● In a large saucepan bring 4 cups *hot water* to boiling. Add pasta and return to boiling. Reduce heat and gently boil for 5 minutes. Then add the frozen vegetables. Return to boiling, then reduce heat. Gently boil about 4 minutes more or till pasta is tender and vegetables are nearly tender. Drain mixture, then return it to the saucepan.

● Add cream cheese and milk. Cook and stir over medium-high heat till cream cheese is melted and mixture is heated through. Season to taste with salt and pepper. Makes 4 servings.

**Making speedy
cheese sauces**

It's quick and easy to make cheese-sauced side dishes when you use a purchased soft cheese product.

Here are two good examples. The sauce for the Peppy Cheese-Sauced Corn is made from a cold-pack cheese food, and the sauce for the Creamy Noodles 'n' Vegetables is made from soft-style cream cheese.

To make the sauces, just stir the cheese product into the hot vegetables or pasta. Then cook till heated through and serve. (Creamy Noodles 'n' Vegetables is shown at right.)

Mayo-Parmesan Bread

For non-garlic lovers, just omit the garlic from this cheesy topper.

1 1-pound loaf unsliced
   French *or* Italian bread
¼ cup grated *or* finely
   shredded Parmesan
   cheese
¼ cup mayonnaise *or* salad
   dressing
1 tablespoon frozen snipped
   chives
¼ teaspoon garlic powder

● Preheat broiler. Meanwhile, cut bread loaf crosswise in half. Reserve half for another use. Then cut remaining bread portion lengthwise in half. Place pieces, cut side up, on the unheated rack of the broiler pan, then set aside.

● In a bowl stir together the Parmesan cheese, mayonnaise or salad dressing, chives, and garlic powder. Spread mixture on bread pieces. Broil bread 4 inches from heat for 2 to 3 minutes or till light brown. Slice to serve. Makes 4 or 5 servings.

Swiss-Almond Crescent Rolls

Try your own variations. Roll up your favorite cheese and nuts in this easy bread fix-up.

1 4-ounce package (4)
   refrigerated crescent rolls
¼ cup shredded Swiss *or*
   cheddar cheese
3 tablespoons sliced almonds

● Preheat oven to 375°. Meanwhile, unroll crescent roll dough and separate into 4 triangles. Place cheese near the wide end of each wedge, then top with the sliced almonds. Beginning at the wide end of each wedge, roll toward the point. Place rolls, point side down, 2 to 3 inches apart on an ungreased baking sheet. Bake rolls in the 375° oven about 12 minutes or till golden. Makes 4 servings.

Bacon-Onion Bubble Bread

Use kitchen shears to quickly cut each biscuit into quarters.

1 tablespoon butter *or*
   margarine
1 4½-ounce package (6)
   refrigerated biscuits
¼ teaspoon onion powder
1 tablespoon cooked bacon
   pieces

● Preheat oven to 450°. Meanwhile, place butter or margarine in an 8-inch round baking pan. Then place the pan in the oven until the butter or margarine is melted.

● While oven is preheating and butter or margarine is melting, cut each biscuit into 4 pieces. Stir onion powder into melted butter or margarine. Then add biscuits. Coat biscuits lightly with butter mixture. Sprinkle with bacon pieces. Bake in the 450° oven for 8 to 10 minutes or till golden. Makes 4 servings.

Cheesy-Herb Bubble Bread: Prepare Bacon-Onion Bubble Bread as above, *except* omit bacon. Stir 1 teaspoon frozen snipped *chives* and ½ teaspoon dried *dillweed or* dried *basil,* crushed along with onion powder into melted butter mixture. Add biscuits and coat. Bake in the 450° oven for 8 to 10 minutes or till golden. Sprinkle with ¼ cup shredded *mozzarella cheese* (1 ounce). Bake about 1 minute more or till cheese is melted.

Banana-Coffee à la Foster

So easy and so good. This banana dessert became a favorite of ours during recipe testing.

Frozen whipped *dairy*
    dessert topping *or* vanilla
    ice cream
4 firm ripe bananas
2 tablespoons lemon juice
¼ cup packed brown sugar
3 tablespoons butter *or*
    margarine
¼ cup Amaretto *or* orange,
    crème d'almond *or* coffee
    liqueur
    Sliced almonds

● If using frozen topping, at the beginning of meal preparation, place it at room temperature to thaw.

● Bias slice bananas into about ½-inch-thick slices. Place the banana slices in a flat dish, then sprinkle with lemon juice. Toss lightly to coat, then set aside till dessert time.

● At dessert time, in a large skillet combine brown sugar and butter or margarine. Cook over medium-high heat till sugar is melted. Remove skillet from heat. Add bananas and liqueur. Return skillet to stove. Cook and gently stir over low heat about 1 minute or till bananas are heated through.

● To serve, spoon the bananas and syrup mixture into dessert dishes, then top with whipped topping and almonds. Or, spoon over ice cream and sprinkle with almonds. Serves 6 to 8.

Skillet Fruit Cobbler

Two good old-fashioned desserts—cobbler and crisp—without fuss.

Frozen whipped *dairy*
    dessert topping, vanilla ice
    cream, *or* light cream
1 21- to 24-ounce can
    blueberry, apple, *or*
    cherry pie filling
1 tablespoon lemon juice
1 tablespoon water
⅓ cup packaged biscuit mix
2 tablespoons broken walnuts
1 tablespoon sugar
⅛ teaspoon cinnamon
4 teaspoons milk

● If using frozen topping, at the beginning of meal preparation, place it at room temperature to thaw.

● In a medium skillet stir together pie filling, lemon juice, and water. Cook over medium-high heat about 5 minutes or till heated through, stirring occasionally. Meanwhile, for biscuit topping, in a mixing bowl stir together biscuit mix, walnuts, sugar, and cinnamon. Add milk, then stir just till combined.

● Spoon biscuit mixture on top of *hot* fruit mixture, making 4 dumplings. Cover skillet and simmer about 7 minutes or till dumplings are done. *(Do not lift lid during cooking.)*

● To serve, spoon filling and dumplings into dessert dishes, then top with whipped topping, ice cream, or cream. Serves 4.

Skillet Fruit Crisp: In a medium skillet heat fruit filling and lemon juice as above, *except* omit water. Meanwhile, for crisp topping, place 1 cup *granola with fruit and nuts, or granola with cinnamon and raisins* in a plastic bag. Close the bag and use a rolling pin to crush the granola. In a small skillet melt 1 tablespoon *butter or margarine.* Stir in 1 tablespoon *sugar*, ⅛ teaspoon ground *cinnamon,* and crushed granola. Sprinkle the topping over warm filling. Then serve as above.

Fruit-Topped Cheesecake

Here's the scoop: This fruit topping is also wonderful over ice cream.

¼ cup red raspberry *or* apricot preserves, *or* strawberry *or* currant jelly

1 cup fresh *or* frozen loose-pack red raspberries, unsweetened whole strawberries, *or* blueberries; *or* frozen loose-pack unsweetened mixed fruit

4 slices deli cheesecake

● In a medium saucepan over medium heat melt preserves or jelly. (Pair raspberries, strawberries, or blueberries with the raspberry preserves, or strawberry or currant jelly. Or, pair the apricot preserves with the mixed fruit.)

● Add fruit and cook about 30 seconds for fresh fruit, or 2 to 3 minutes for frozen fruit or till thawed. Chill the topping while eating dinner. Serve topping over cheesecake. Serves 4.

Cocoa-Nutty Sauce

For an even nuttier flavor, add chopped peanuts.

¾ cup sugar

⅓ cup unsweetened cocoa powder

1 5-ounce can (⅔ cup) evaporated milk

¼ cup chunky peanut butter

2 to 3 tablespoons milk (optional)

Ice cream

● In a saucepan combine sugar and cocoa. Stir in evaporated milk. Cook and stir over medium-high heat for 3 to 4 minutes or till thickened and slightly bubbly. Remove from heat. Stir in peanut butter. Cover to keep warm while eating dinner.

● To serve, if necessary, stir milk into sauce to make of desired consistency. Spoon sauce over ice cream. Makes 1⅓ cups sauce.

To micro-cook: In a microwave-safe mixing bowl or 4-cup measure stir together sugar and cocoa powder. Then stir in evaporated milk. Micro-cook, uncovered, on 100% power (high) for 2 to 3 minutes or till boiling, stirring once. Then stir in peanut butter. Cover and let stand while eating dinner. Serve as above.

Sparkling Fruit

For a refreshingly icy dessert, make sure the fruit is only partially thawed.

1 10-ounce package frozen light-syrup-pack mixed fruit, strawberries, *or* red raspberries (in quick-thaw pouch)

1 teaspoon lemon juice *or* 4 teaspoons Amaretto

½ cup ginger ale

● Just before eating dinner, place frozen fruit at room temperature to *partially* thaw.

● At dessert time, spoon partially thawed fruit into wineglasses or sherbet dishes. Add about ¼ *teaspoon* of the lemon juice or *1 teaspoon* Amaretto to *each* glass of fruit. Then add *2 tablespoons* ginger ale to *each* glass of fruit. Makes 4 servings.

Fruit-Topped Cheesecake
(red raspberry version)

(blueberry version)

(mixed-fruit version)

Fresh Fruit 'n' Cream

In winter try this Amaretto-cream-cheese topping on sliced bananas or canned sliced peaches.

½ of an 8-ounce container of soft-style cream cheese
2 tablespoons milk
1 tablespoon powdered sugar
1 tablespoon Amaretto
2 cups small strawberries, blueberries, red raspberries, *or* a combination
2 tablespoons sliced almonds

● In a small mixing bowl use a rotary beater to beat cream cheese, milk, powdered sugar, and Amaretto till well combined.

● To serve, place fruit into dessert dishes. Top with cream cheese mixture, then sprinkle with almonds. Makes 4 servings.

Orange Ice-Cream Dreamers

2 orange slices (optional)
1 pint (2 cups) vanilla ice cream
½ cup orange juice
⅓ cup peach schnapps *or* Amaretto

● If using orange slices for garnish, cut them in half and set aside. In a blender container or food processor bowl place ice cream, orange juice, and schnapps or Amaretto. Cover and blend or process just till smooth. Pour into champagne or wineglasses to serve. Garnish with oranges. Serves 4.

Chocolate-Mint Ice-Cream Dreamers: Omit orange. In a blender container or food processor bowl place 1 pint (2 cups) *chocolate ice cream,* ¼ cup *crème de cacao* liqueur, and ¼ cup white *crème de menthe* liqueur. Blend and serve as above.

7-Minute Mocha Mousse

1 8-ounce container of frozen whipped *dairy* dessert topping
1 tablespoon milk
2 teaspoons instant coffee crystals
⅓ cup fudge ice-cream topping
Pirouettes (rolled sugar cookies) (optional)

● At the beginning of meal preparation, place frozen topping at room temperature to thaw. Meanwhile, in a medium bowl combine milk and coffee crystals. Let stand for 2 to 3 minutes or till crystals are dissolved. Stir in fudge topping.

● Before serving, fold the thawed whipped dessert topping into the fudge mixture. Spoon mixture into dessert dishes or wineglasses. If desired, serve with cookies. Makes 6 servings.

7-Minute Fudge-Orange Mousse: Prepare 7-Minute Mocha Mousse as above, *except* omit milk, coffee, and cookies. Stir 1 tablespoon frozen *orange juice concentrate* into fudge topping. Fold in whipped topping. Spoon into dishes. If desired, garnish with canned, drained *mandarin orange sections.*

Index

Index

If you're like most busy people today, you don't have a lot of time to spend in the kitchen. For dozens of easy, quick-to-fix recipes that'll fit into your active life-style, turn to the BETTER HOMES AND GARDENS® *In-a-Hurry Cook Book* and the *On-the-Go Cook Book.*